THE GREAT MASTERS OF ART

# FRIDA KAHLO

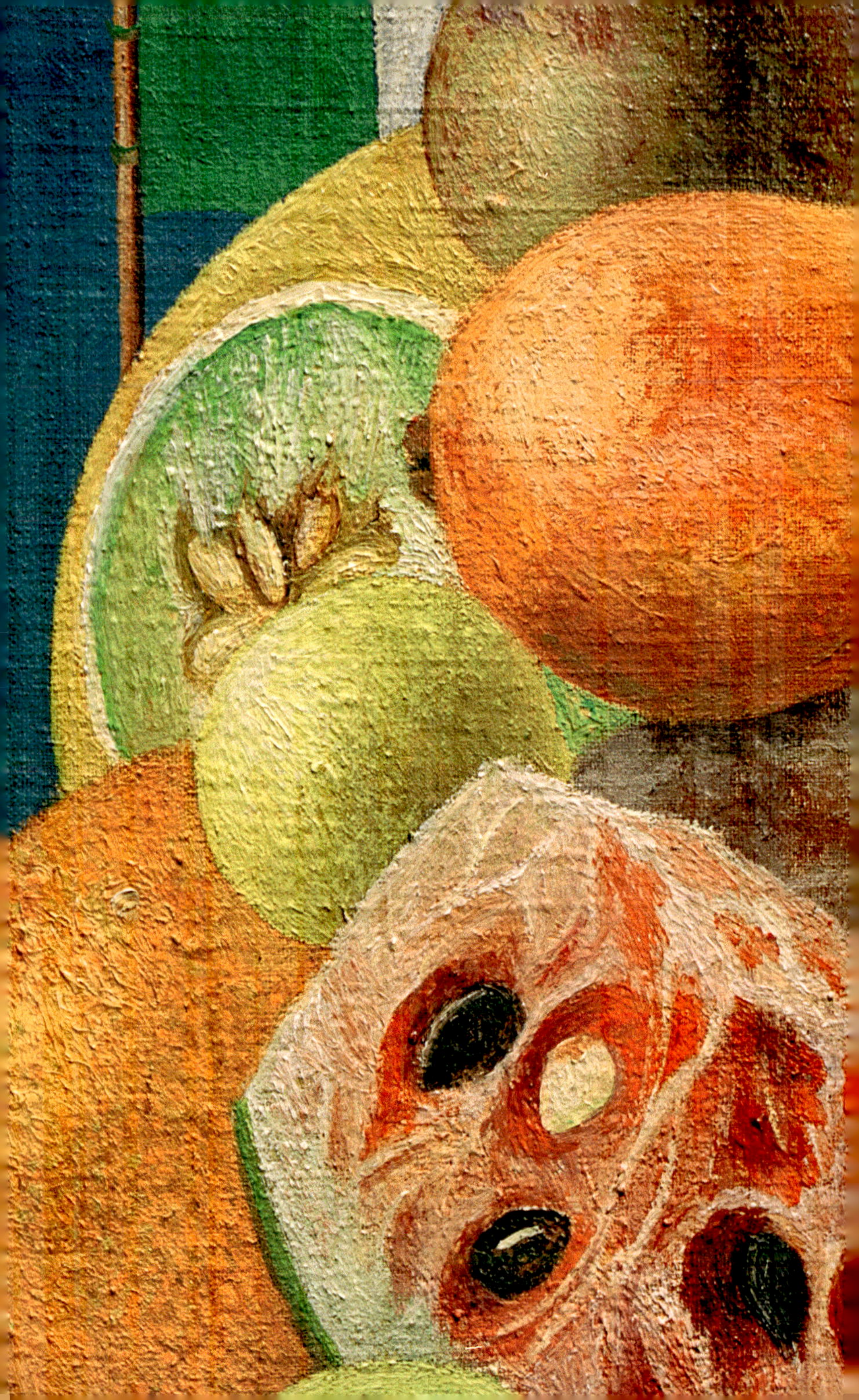

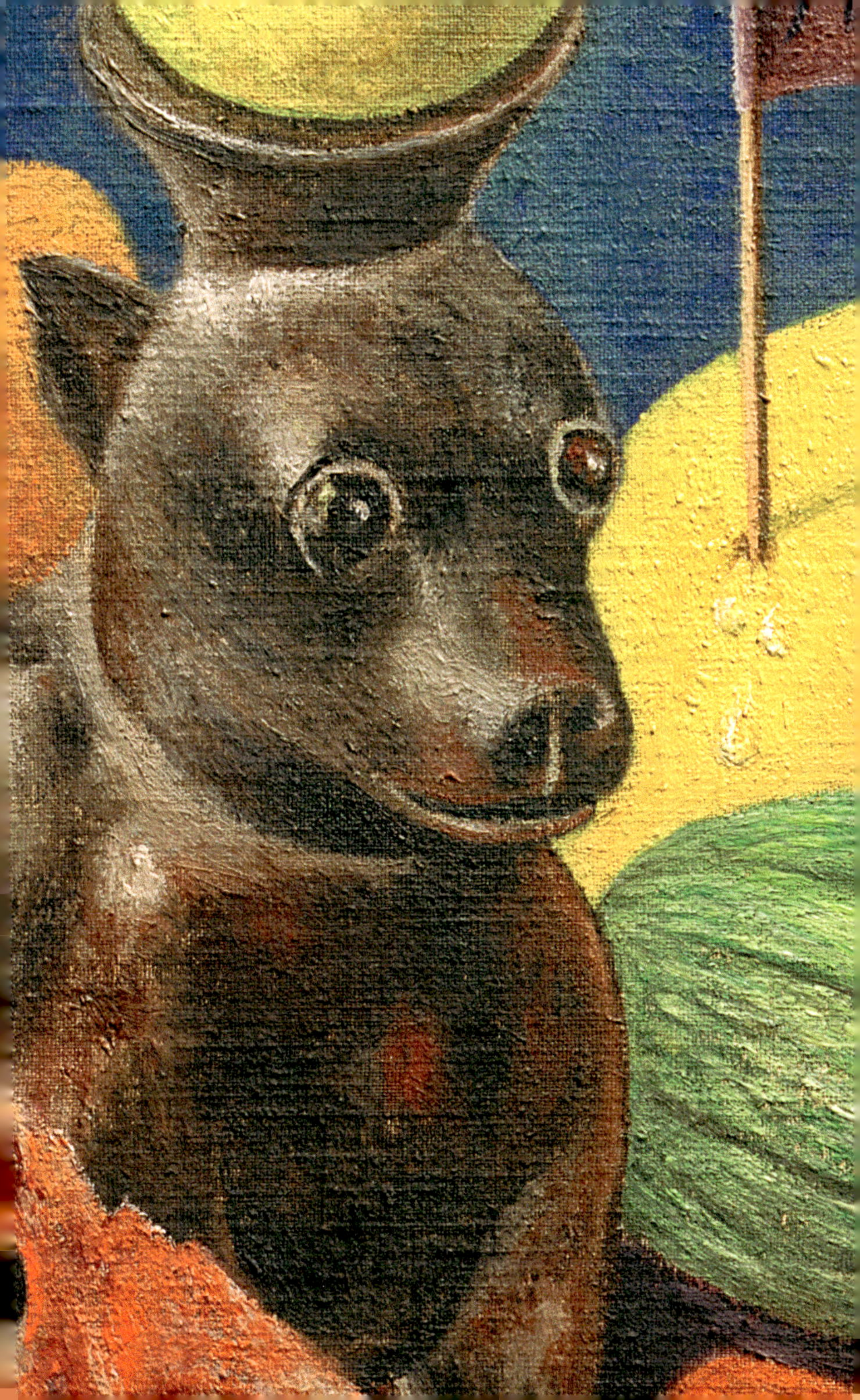

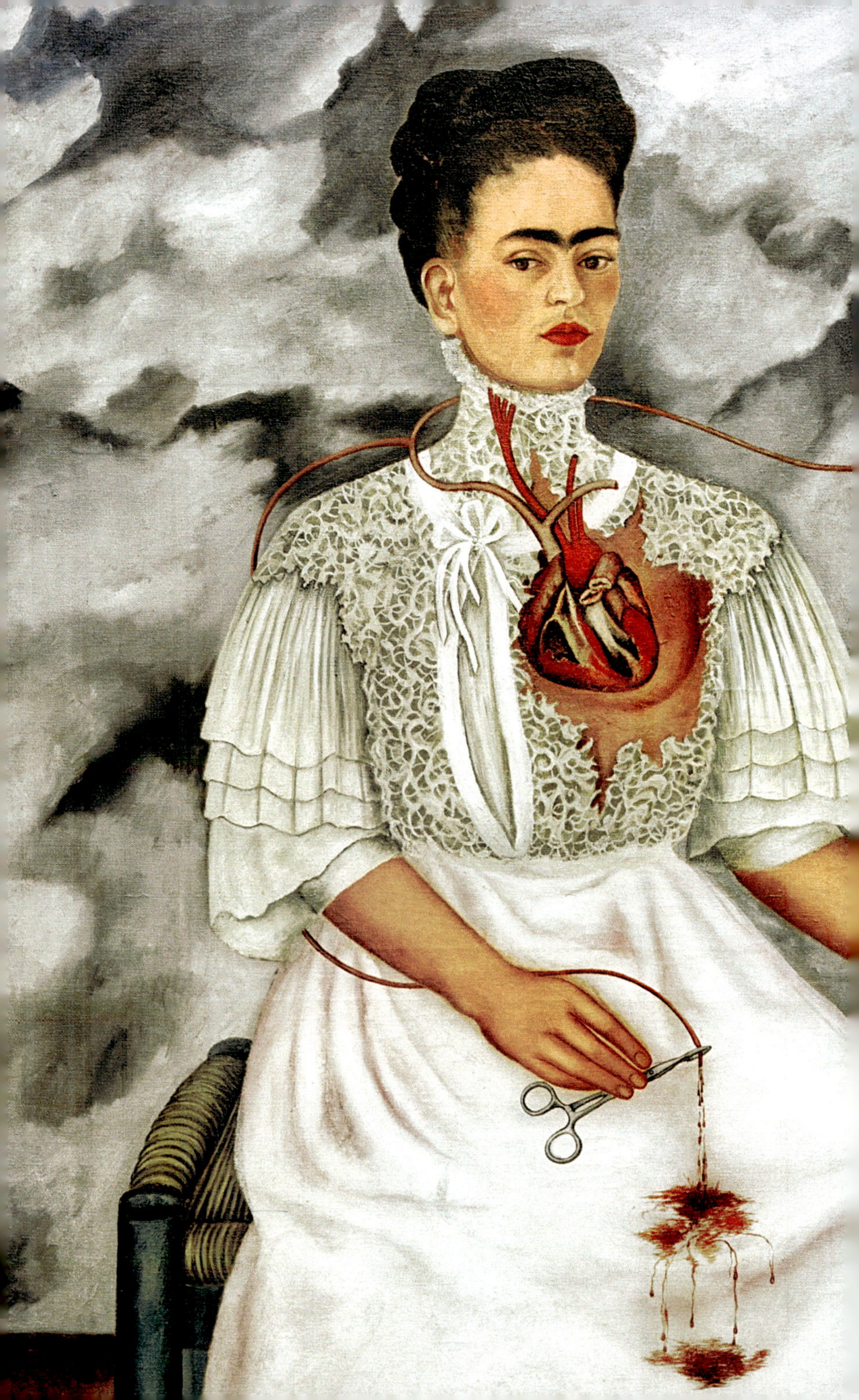

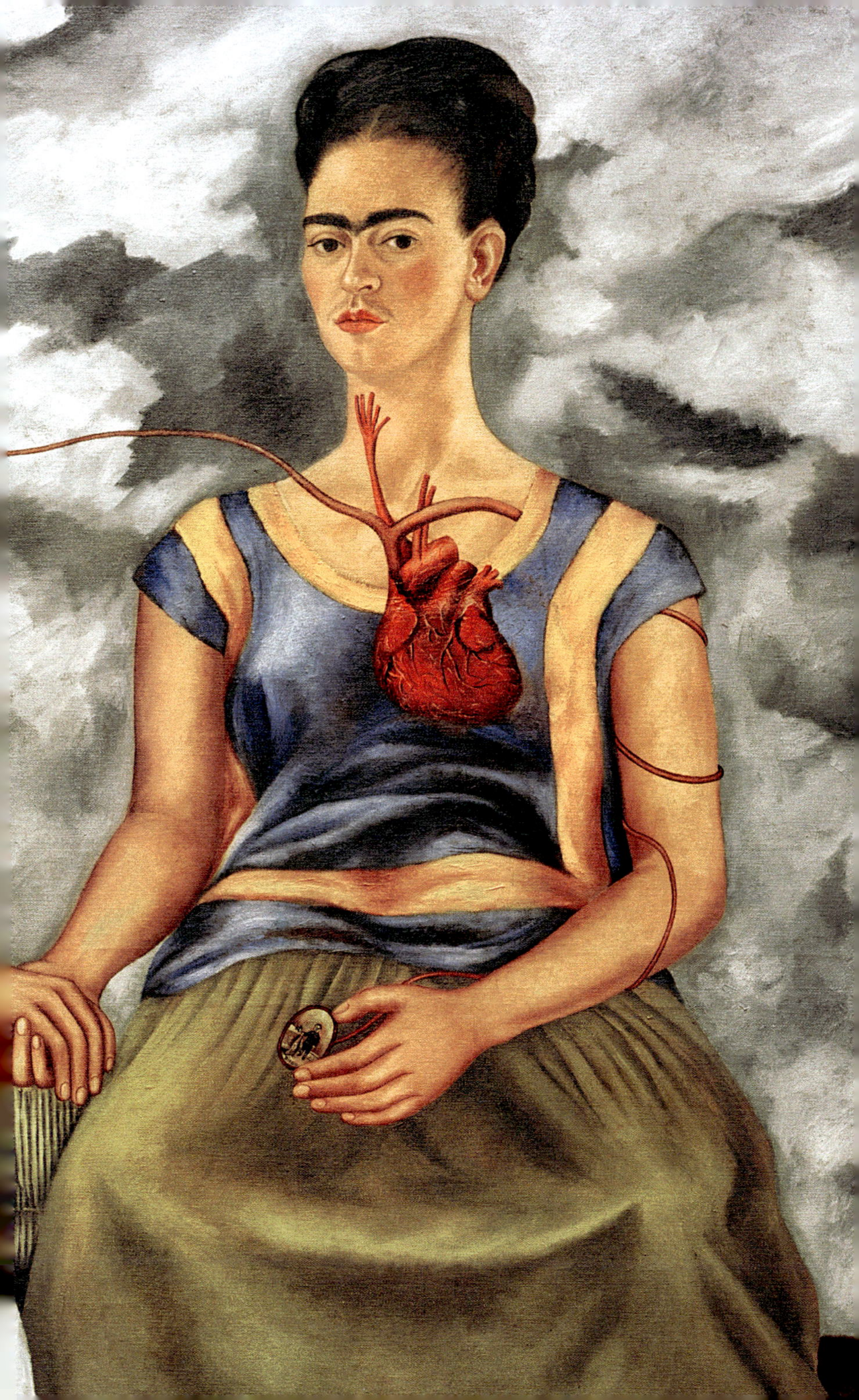

# FRIDA
# KAHLO

Teresa Grenzmann

HIRMER

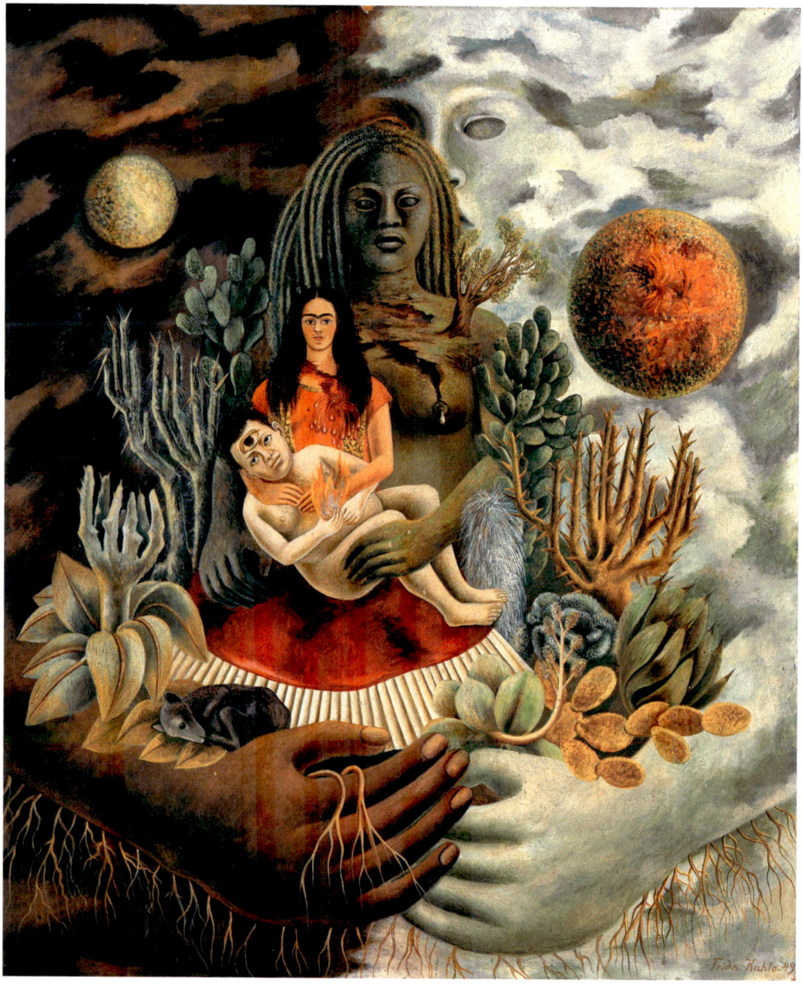

**FRIDA KAHLO**

*The Love Embrace of the Universe, Earth (Mexico), I, Diego, and Mr. Xólotl,* 1949, oil on hardboard, 70 × 60.5 cm
Jacques and Natasha Gelman Collection, Mexico City

# CONTENTS

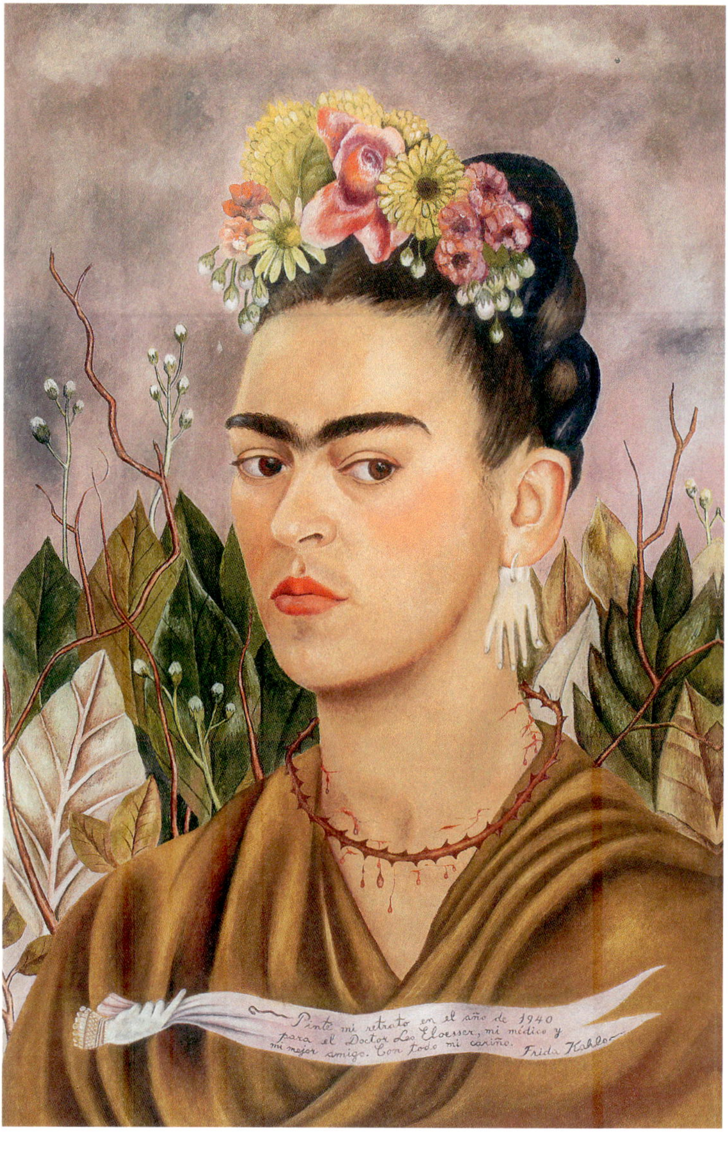


1 *Self-Portrait, Dedicated to Dr Eloesser,* 1940, oil on Masonite, 59.5 × 40 cm, Private collection

# FRIDA IN THE MIRROR

Teresa Grenzmann

In 1939 Frida Kahlo gave two almost identical frames as a gift to her friend Mary Sklar. The first one contained one of her self-portraits with monkeys. Composed of thousands of the finest, most patient brushstrokes, it nevertheless emanates a rarely tranquil, peaceful, pastel softness, despite the invariably proud, sublime gaze of Frida. The second frame, somewhat larger, depicts the observer: reflected in a mirror.

It is not art, but clearly the gesture to her close New York friend instead that makes this mirror necessary for Frida Kahlo. When she exhibited the picture in the Julien Levy Gallery in early November 1938, it was hung, like all the others, by itself. Kahlo alone. Kahlo, who lived with her loneliness and at the same time struggled against it, who addressed it in her pictures and simultaneously despaired of it. "I paint self-portraits because I am so often alone," she said, "because I am the person that I know best."[1] Now she declared to Mary Sklar that in this way she and Kahlo could be together always.

So the mirror in *Fulang Chang and I* (2) was also originally an intimate message of affection—and an expression of a deep wish. In the setting of the Museum of Modern Art in New York, where both paintings are displayed next to each other, they signal to the visitor personal closeness,

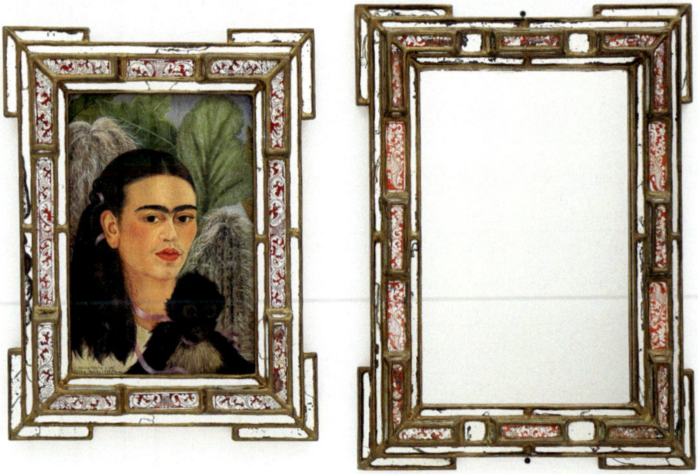

2 *Fulang Chang and I*, 1937, oil on hardboard, 40 × 28 cm, painted frame with mirror added after 1939, 56.5 × 44.1 cm, Museum of Modern Art, New York



creating identification through contemplation, and reflecting back what has defined the fascination—in fact, the cult—of the woman and painter Frida Kahlo since her rediscovery in the 1980s: Kahlo, lonely throughout her entire life, became famous after her death, an international star and a feminist idol.

In the search for the origin of this fascination, the mirror remains a central motif. It appears in Kahlo's childhood, in her adolescence, many times in her suffering, in her marriage with Diego Rivera, in her artistic work of course, and in her œuvre's omnipresent self-centeredness. A life surrounded by mirrors—in many ways.

## BEGINNINGS: THE PORTRAIT AS SUBSTITUTE

Frida Kahlo's father Guillermo was actually called Wilhelm Kahlo. In 1891, when he was nineteen, he emigrated from Pforzheim in Germany to Mexico City, began working for a photographer there, and in 1898 married the photographer's daughter, Matilde Calderón y Gonzales. That same year he opened a studio. Soon he could afford to buy a property in Coyoacán, a wealthy suburb. There he had the famous Blue House, "La Casa Azul," built. It was here that Magdalena Carmen Frieda Kahlo y Calderón was born on July 6, 1907.

From now on, the photographic eye of his camera was the first mirror in Kahlo's life. While outside the revolution raged bloodily, Guillermo captured Frida in pretty children's photos. He made his daughter familiar with posing, with her self-image, her impact. But also—when Kahlo was old enough to assist him—with attentive looking and detailed drawing, with precise studies and great care.

We know from her diary that Kahlo cultivated a "magical friendship" at the age of six.[2] This imaginary female friend was a mirrored self, a door to the world of her imagination, a counterpart that would later be closely linked to her search for identity in the role-playing between Mexican and European roots, loving wife and emancipated painter, *alegría* (cheerfulness) and the pain of life, self-expression, and self-doubt. In her work, this alter ego would recur, for example, in the large painting *The Two Fridas* (3), and in *Tree of Hope* (4), when the healthy Frida Kahlo keeps watch next to the sick one. "She was her beginning and her end," writes Kahlo's biographer Hayden Herrera, "her creator, her nurturer, and her destroyer."[3]

It was probably around this time, when Frida was seven or eight, that she suffered an illness or injury, usually diagnosed as polio but more recently attributed to a congenital malformation of the spine (spina bifida). From that time onward Kahlo had problems with her right leg. It was thinner and shorter than the other one, a fact which she tried to conceal with stockings and later under the long skirts of her Tehuana costume. She walked with a limp and was teased. Kahlo disregarded this, yet suffered from it.

A drawing for a classmate by the twelve-year-old Frida can be considered her first self-portrait. The comment with which she demanded attention even then is striking: "I am sending you my portrait here so that you will remember me."[4]

When Frida Kahlo entered high school to prepare for medical studies, the fifteen-year-old was one of the first thirty-five girls admitted to the Escuela Nacional Preparatoria. But she deliberately set herself apart through her masculine appearance. She soon joined the rebellious "Cachuchas" group

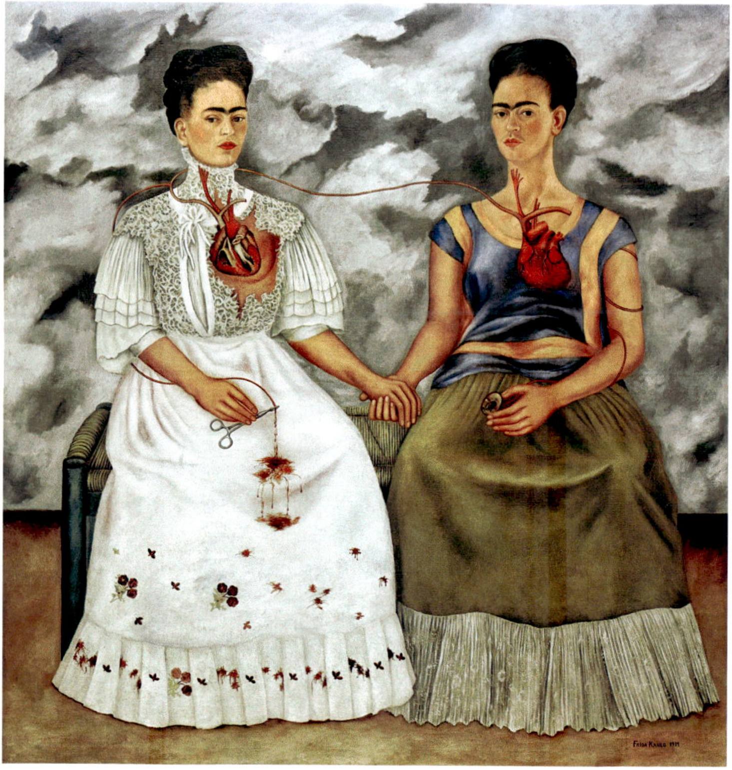

**3** *The Two Fridas,* 1939, oil on canvas, 173.5 × 173 cm, Museo de Arte Moderno, Mexico City

and fell in love with its leader, Alejandro Gómez Arias. Together with him, on September 17, 1925, she experienced the tragic accident that would define her life: A streetcar rammed the bus in which she was sitting; a holding rod pierced her abdomen, and she suffered severe injuries and fractures to her spine, ribs, collarbone, pelvis, right leg, and foot. There is a story that in the confusion someone shouted "¡La bailarina!" (The dancer!), because gold dust, apparently from another passenger's luggage, covered her bloody body. The myth of Frida Kahlo.

"I didn't die, and besides, I have something worth living for: painting."[5] A plaster corset now enclosed the eighteen-year-old's torso "from her collarbone to her pelvis." Because Frida was bored in her hospital bed, her

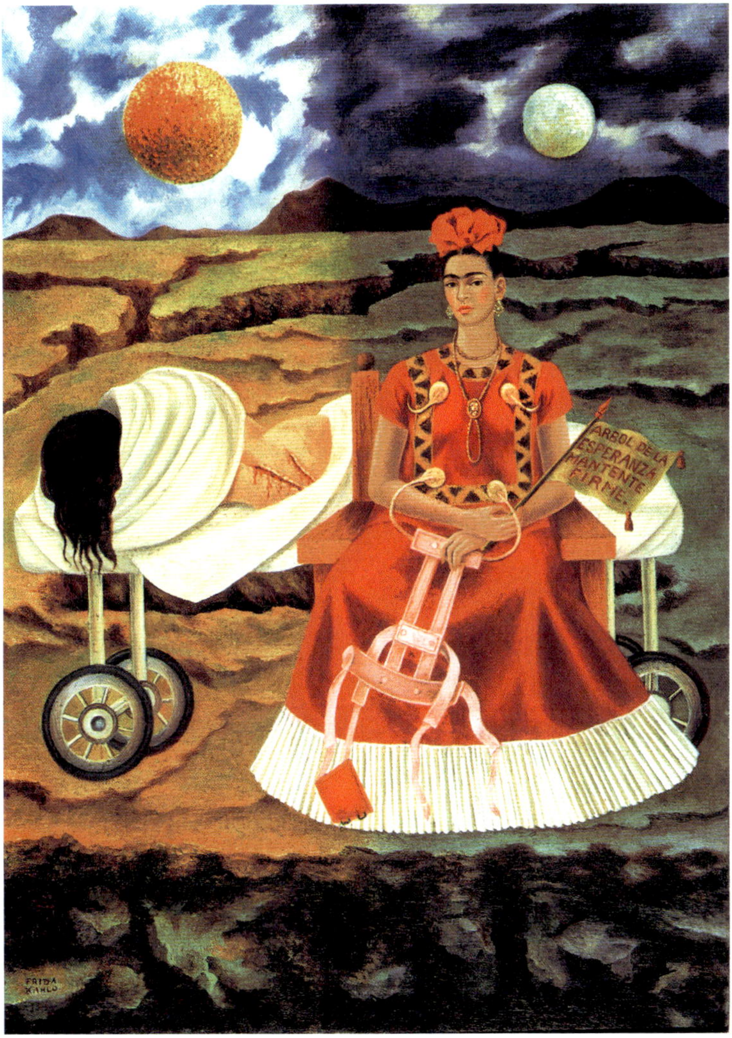


**4** *Tree of Hope,* 1946, oil on Masonite, Private collection

mother constructed an easel for her. "She attached a canopy," Kahlo recalls, "and hung a mirror on the underside so I could use my reflection as a model."[6] Kahlo gave her first painted, still very flat, *Self-Portrait Wearing a Velvet Dress* (5) to Alejandro Gómez Arias, self-indulgently calling it "Your Botticeli" [sic] in admiration of the Italian Renaissance painters, and asking in a letter, "I beg you to hang it low, so you can see it as if you were looking at me."[7]

**5** *Self-Portrait Wearing a Velvet Dress,* 1926, oil on canvas, 79.7 × 59.9 cm
Private collection

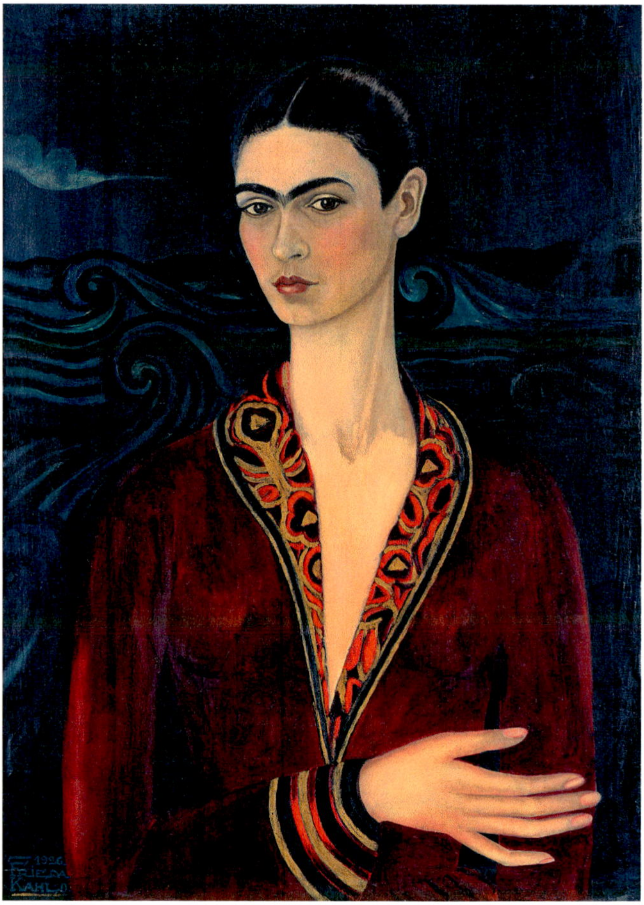

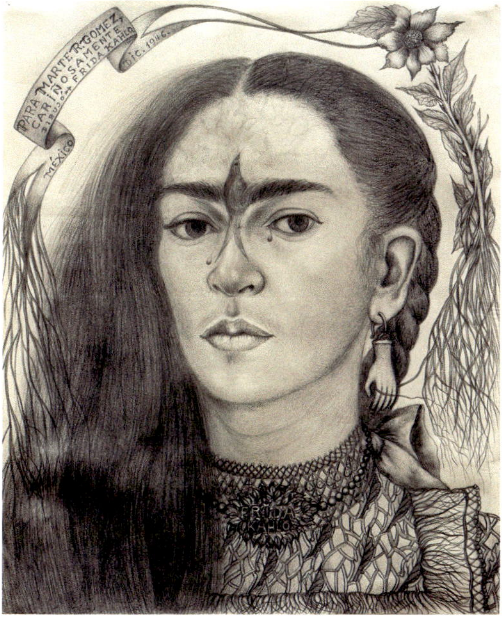


*6 Self-Portrait, Dedicated to Marte R. Gómez,* 1946
Pencil on paper, 38.5 × 32.5 cm, Private collection

The portrait as a proxy. At this early point in her life, the desire for a dialogue through her art arose out of the loneliness of the illness. Her first love already turned into a passionate, voluble struggle for closeness, into that dependence on attention and recognition that would last her entire life.

## SELF-PORTRAIT: THE SELF IN THE MIRROR

In front of her father's lens, Frida Kahlo displayed herself on one and the same day in 1926 in a neat girl's dress and in a correct man's suit—stiff and thoughtful (33). A groping for an expression of otherness, emancipation, and rebellion. Her face already expressed the serious, proud composure with which she would gaze out at the viewer in her paintings and drawings from now on, even when tears welled up in her eyes, as in the memorable pencil drawing dedicated to Marte R. Gómez from December 1946, in which she is composed of a natural and a coiffed half of her head (6). Or

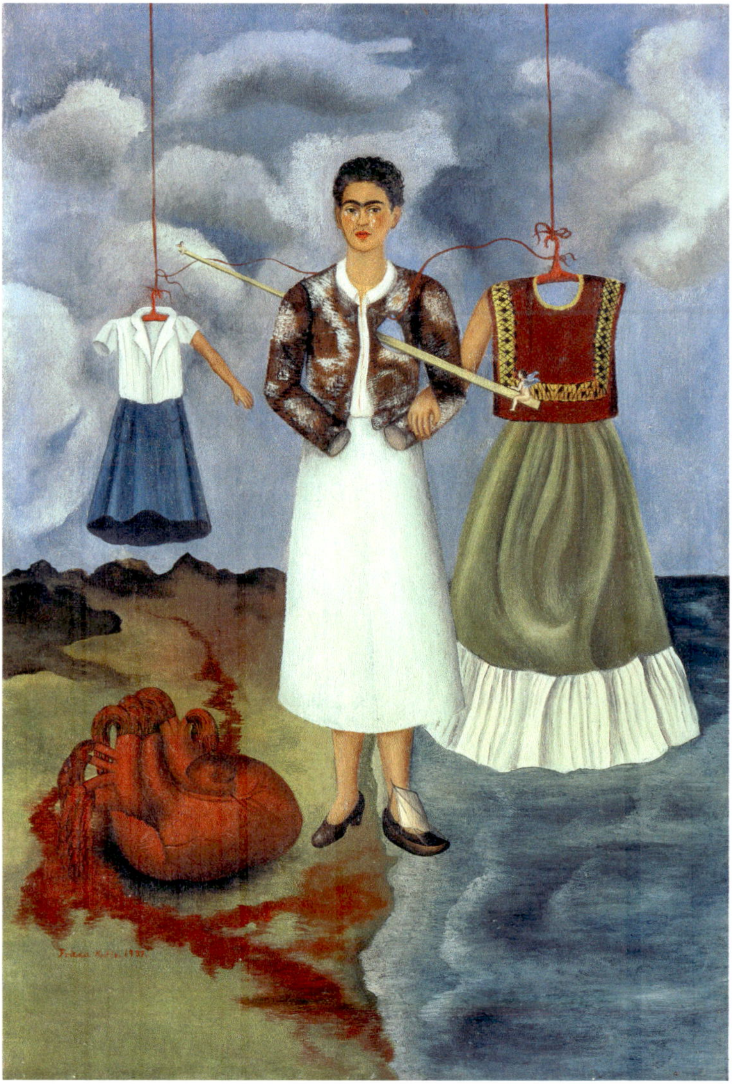

7 *Memory, The Heart*, 1937, oil on metal, 40 × 28 cm, Private collection

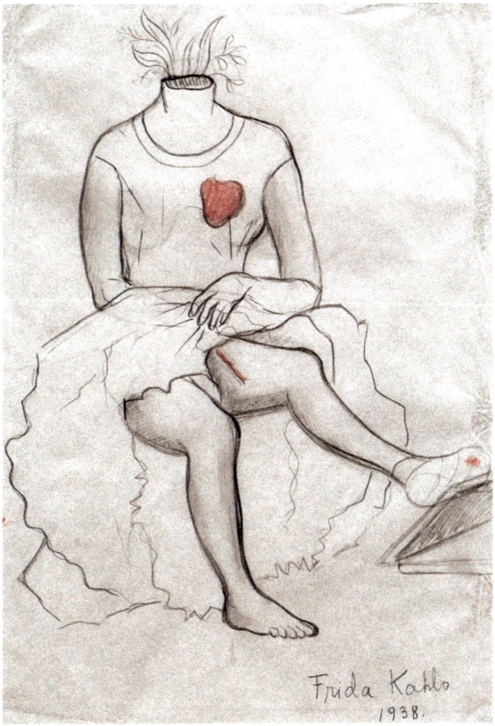


**8** *Self-Portrait Showing the Scar*, 1938, pencil and colored pencil on paper 28.6 × 19.7 cm, Private collection

in 1948, when she frames her face with a traditional *resplandor*, the Mexican headdress for special occasions: Kahlo weeps without emotion—the tears are symbols of her suffering.

In *The Memory, The Heart* (7) from 1937, she weeps over the affair of her husband Diego Rivera, Mexico's most famous painter, whom she married in 1929, with her favorite sister Cristina, who was only eleven months younger. In the rift between the little girl's German school uniform and the married woman's costume, Kahlo's handless, powerless figure embodies an enormous sense of loss. What is depicted nevertheless remains an image; the image remains an illustration, and emotions explain themselves in symbols, preventing identification and compassion. In three drawings from the same period, Kahlo even plays with the unmasking of her self-dramatization: in *Drawing a Self-Portrait* (c. 1937), five arms are busy arranging her appearance while she paints herself with a sixth hand.

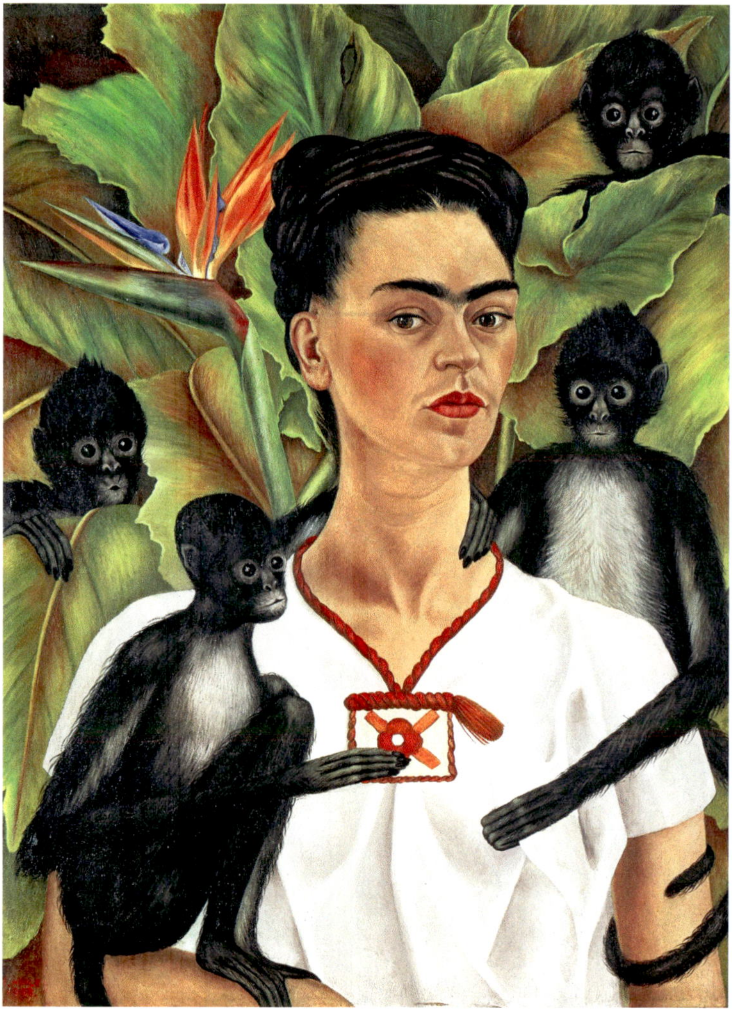

9 *Self-Portrait with Monkeys,* 1943, oil on canvas, 81.5 × 63 cm
Jacques and Natasha Gelman Collection, Mexico City

In *Remembrance of an Open Wound* (1938) and *Self-Portrait Showing the Scar* (8), she pulls up her costume to expose her injuries.

Kahlo painted portraits of women from the ordinary population of Mexico, of family members, friends, doctors, supporters. However, the focus of her œuvre, which encompassed more than 200 works between 1926 and 1954, is clearly on self-portraiture. Hayden Herrera, whose 1983 publication was instrumental in rescuing the artist from oblivion, refers to these self-portraits as "permanently-made mirror images."[8] They provide Kahlo with a controlled, abstractly naive to mask-like, (magically) realistic to surrealistic projection surface for her experiences and inner life. They signify reflection (as self-assurance and self-manifestation) just as much as performance (in varying costumes), and at times also political commentary. "My painting conceals the message of pain. […] It is not revolutionary—why do I still hope it is militant; I cannot."[9]

Frida Kahlo as a fighter—this is how she was perceived by others. Diego Rivera portrayed his wife as a determined communist in his murals depicting a social utopia; photographs record her demonstrating alongside him; and she confidently showed herself with Leon Trotsky when he arrived in his Mexican exile with his wife in 1937 to stay at the Blue House. Eleven days before her death, on July 2, 1954, she left her bed, despite pneumonia, to protest in a wheelchair with a raised fist against the deposing of Guatemalan President Jacobo Árbenz Guzmán. Her painting might not seem revolutionary (enough) to her—but already then her impact was.

## TOGETHER: LOVE AND BE LOVED

Frida Kahlo met Diego Rivera in 1928 while she was still at the Preparatoria. Here she asked the famous muralist, who had just returned from a long sojourn in Europe and was on his scaffolding, working on the mural *The Creation* in the auditorium, to look at some of her pictures. She painted primarily for pleasure, she explained, but wanted later to earn a living from it.[10] He encouraged her. On August 21, 1929, Kahlo and Rivera married; she was twenty-two, he forty-two. Rivera was also the one who recommended that she concentrate on the subject of self-reflection.

In the deep pain of a miscarriage—which Rivera, who wanted no more children, did not share with her—Kahlo painted both the associative (nightmare) dream paintings *Henry Ford Hospital* and *Frida and the Miscarriage* (10), as well as the dramatic double self-portrait *My Birth* (1932). For the first time, she used her art to catalyze her feelings and emphatically make them public. The naivety of the representation makes what is depicted seem less drastic. Surrounded by two-dimensional emptiness, later often against the background of a barren wasteland, displayed like an object without light or shadow, she depicts herself as vulnerable and strong at the same time. In this she draws on the religious tradition of ex-voto images on simple, small-format metal panels. In the Blue House, which is today the home of the Frida Kahlo Museum, there are walls with hundreds of such *retablos*, amateurish images usually dedicated to saints in gratitude for a life that was saved or an illness that was healed. In *My Birth* these thanks are sarcastically subverted: Kahlo, feeling as if she has died, paints herself as a dead mother and as her dead child, replacing the mother's head with the icon of a mater dolorosa.

Kahlo would often portray herself as a Madonna. The baby Jesus is replaced by dolls (17) or by the little monkeys with whom she surrounded herself in tender affection in Coyoacán. Even "Dieguito," whom she often referred to as her child and showered with almost maternal love, is cradled in her lap as a giant baby in her complex painting of the origin of all being, *The Love Embrace of the Universe, Earth (Mexico), I, Diego and Mr. Xólotl* (p. 8). "Frida is the only person I know who brought herself into being by her own will," a close friend recalled, "she is the only person who gave birth to herself."[11]

With her marriage, Kahlo's outward transformation began; she traded in her tomboyish work overalls for the lush, colorful clothing worn by women in the matriarchal society on the Isthmus of Tehuantepec. She also exchanged her chummy attitude towards the male world for the feminine charms of the *gran ocultadora*, the seductively mysterious woman. The gazes of others acted as a mirror through which Kahlo was seen. From now on, her exterior was juxtaposed with her interior. When she accompanied Rivera to the United States from November 1930 to the end of 1933, where he worked on commissions in San Francisco, Detroit (for Henry Ford), and New York (for Nelson Rockefeller), the *mexicanidad*, so carefully celebrated every day and staged as a total work of art, evolved into Kahlo's

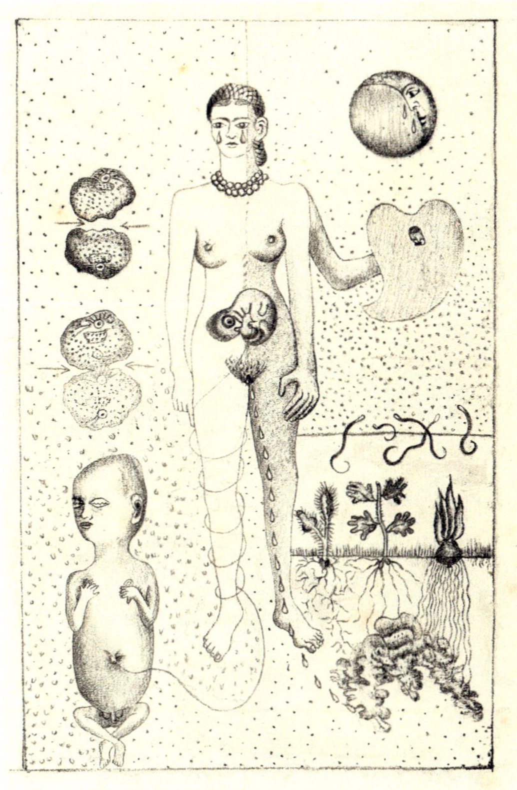

**10** *Frida and the Miscarriage*, 1932
Lithograph on paper
22.5 × 14.5 cm
Private collection

sensational trademark. She combined traditional Mexican garments such as embroidered blouses and lace-trimmed skirts, cotton tunics, and crocheted scarves, but also bought Chinese fabrics, designed dresses and rings, strung pre-Columbian tools and jade beads as well as gemstones, coral, and silver into heavy necklaces, and devoted much time to her braided hairstyles interwoven with ribbons. Critical pictures such as the collage *My Dress Hangs There* (11) or her *Self-Portrait on the Borderline Between Mexico and the United States* (12), on the other hand, reveal her malaise amidst the discrepancy between materialism and poverty in "Gringolandia."

At the same time, Kahlo made herself small at Rivera's side. In her simple wedding portrait she almost disappears next to the powerful figure of her

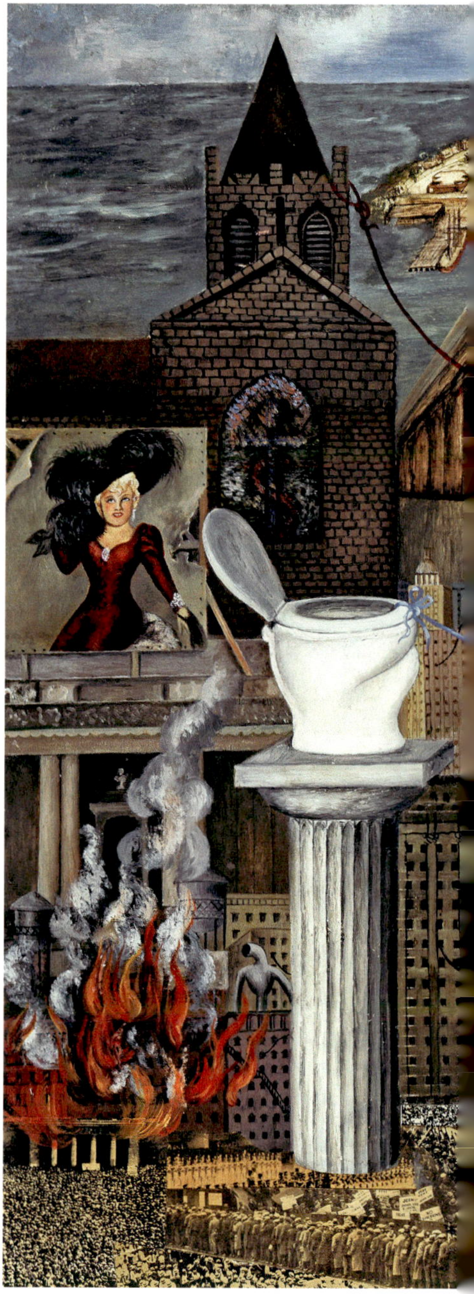

11 *My Dress Hangs There,* 1933
Oil and collage on hard fiber
46 × 49.5 cm, Private collection

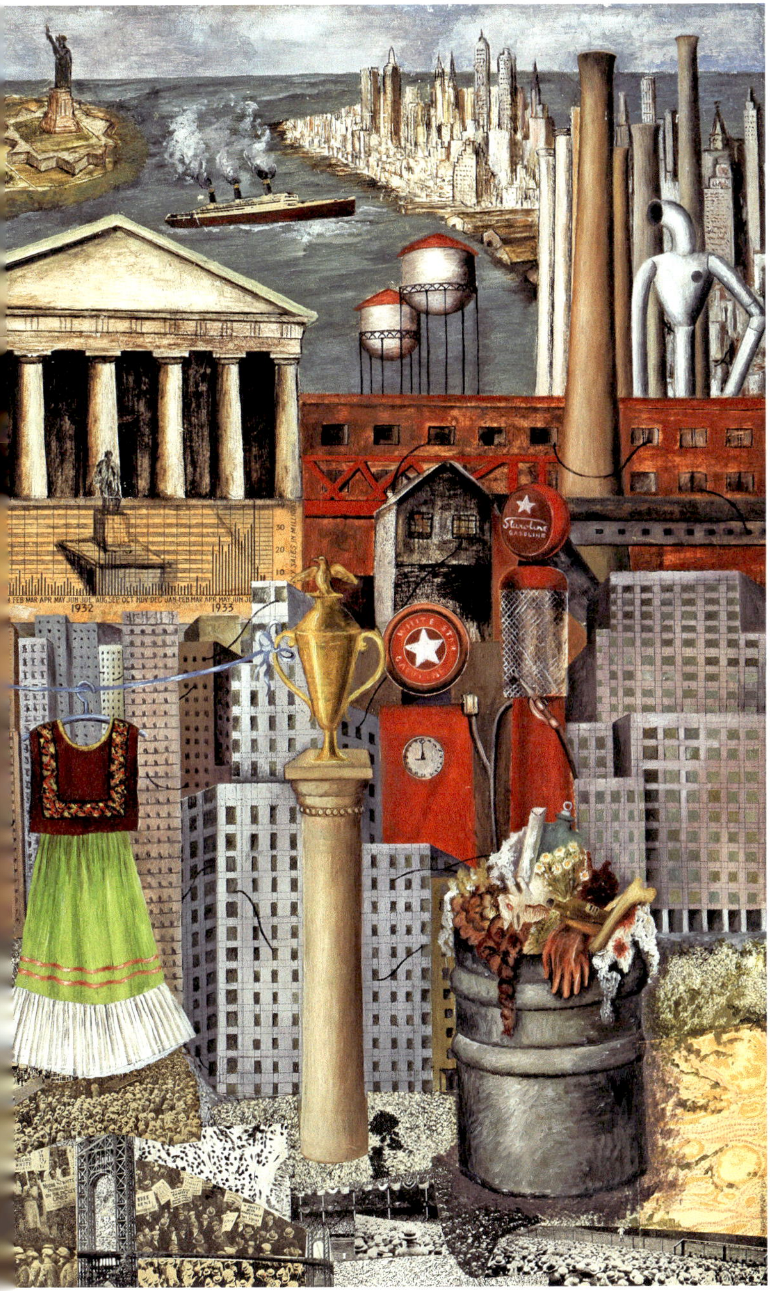
1932
1933

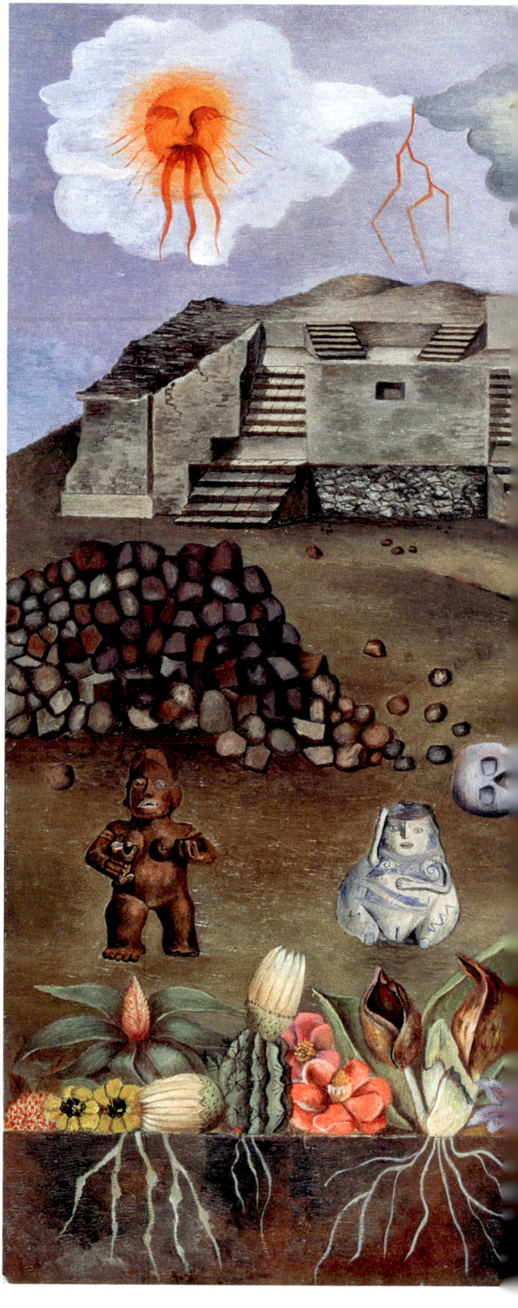

12 *Self-Portrait on the Borderline Between Mexico and the United States,* 1932
Oil on metal, 31 × 35 cm
Private collection

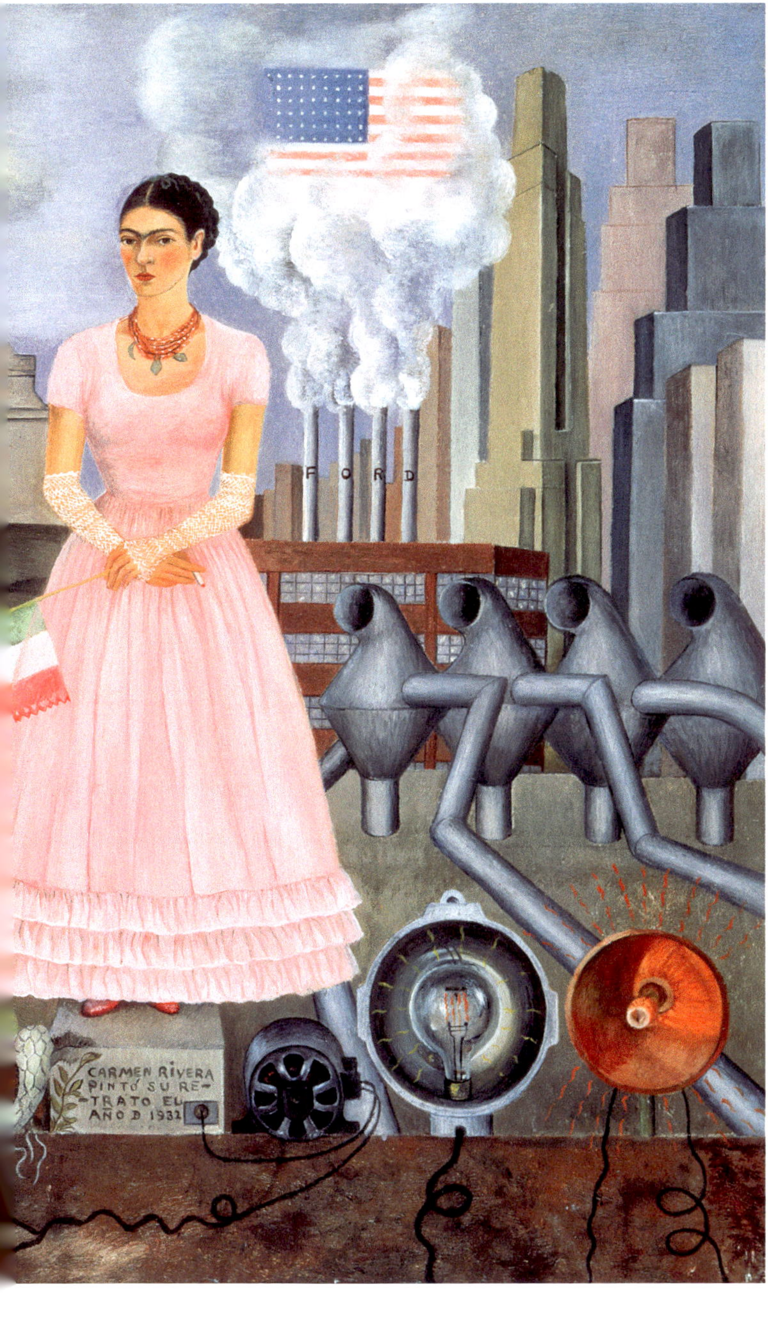
FORD
CARMEN RIVERA
PINTÓ SU RE-
-TRATO EL
AÑO D 1932

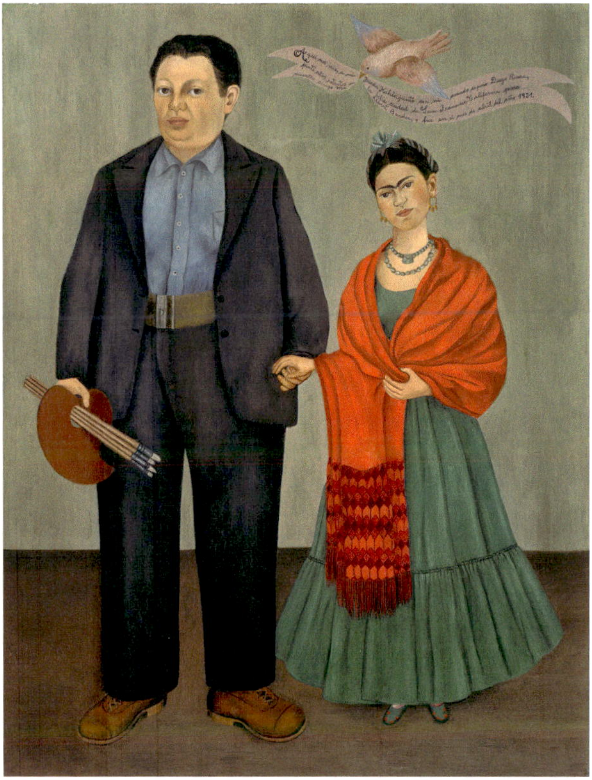

**13** *Frida and Diego Rivera,* 1931, oil on canvas, 100 × 78.7 cm
San Francisco Museum of Modern Art



husband (13); in her letters she belittles herself as "Friducha" or "chiquita." In her diary she laments to him that she is lonely, imbuing him with the ability to counteract it as a strong "tree of hope," as a "formidable column that is the basis of the entire human structure,"[12] and sighs, "Diego is the name of love."[13]

Her whole life was defined by two poles: loving and suffering. This was also made clear in the numerous letters to her close friend, Dr. Leo Eloesser in San Francisco, a physician specializing in thoracic surgery, to whom she confided eloquently over a period of twenty-four years (1). However, this incessant interplay between happiness and pain, appreciation and repulsion was personified by the man with whom she was in daily intellectual

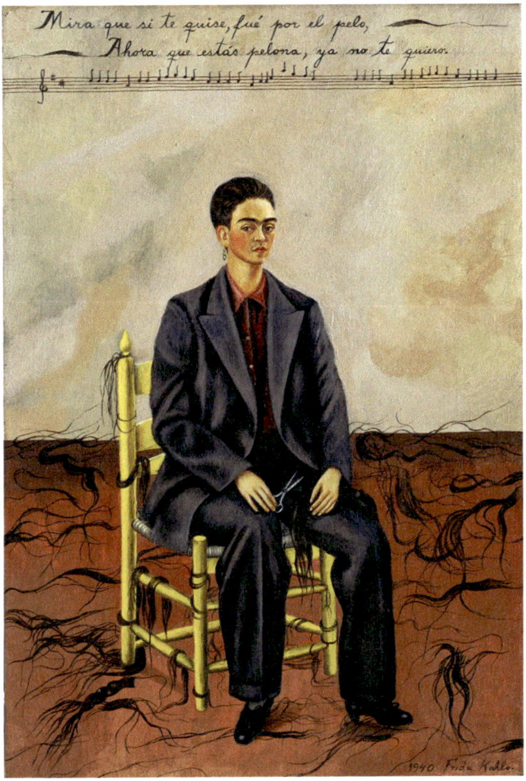


**14** *Self-Portrait with Cropped Hair,* 1940, oil on canvas
40 × 28.5 cm, Museum of Modern Art, New York

contact: Diego Rivera. In the context of her social and political commitment, Kahlo unconditionally supported him when he was expelled from the Communist Party during the Rockefeller scandal in New York, and when he was accused of helping to assassinate Trotsky.

Returning from the United States, the two moved into their new semi-detached house in the San Angel quarter at the end of 1933: two modern cubes, connected only by a narrow footbridge. When Rivera cheated on her with her sister Cristina shortly thereafter, Frida Kahlo defiantly discarded her traditional costume and cropped her hair short (14). For the first time, she played with the idea of taking her own life. In 1935 she moved alone to the center of Mexico City, and in early July she took a trip

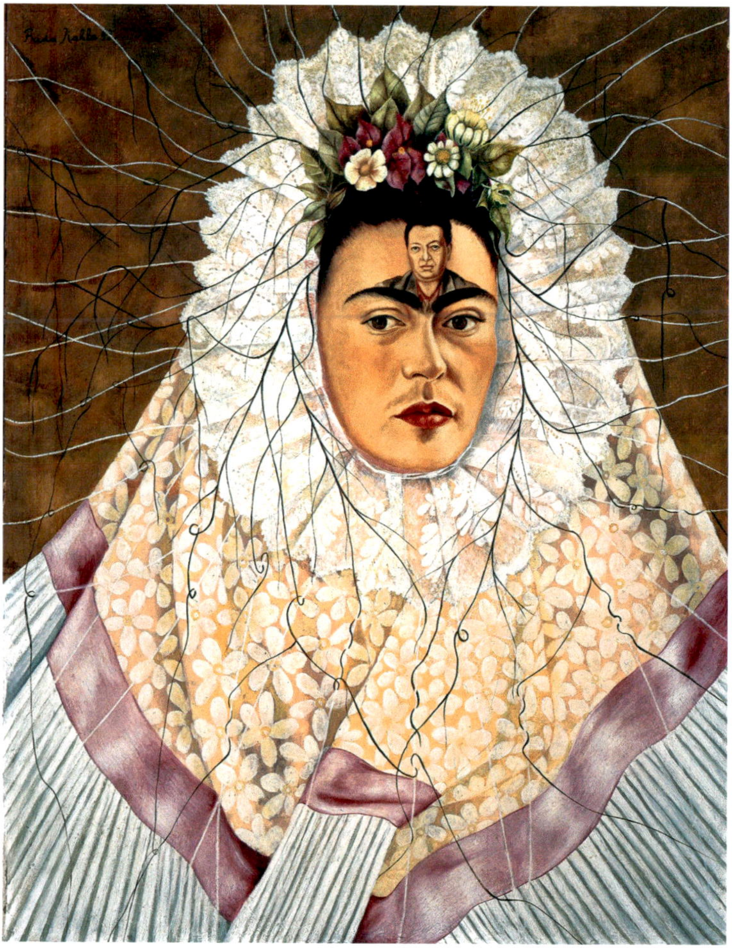

15 *Self-Portrait as Tehuana (Diego in My Thoughts)*, 1943, oil on hardboard, 76 × 61 cm
Jacques and Natasha Gelman Collection, Mexico City

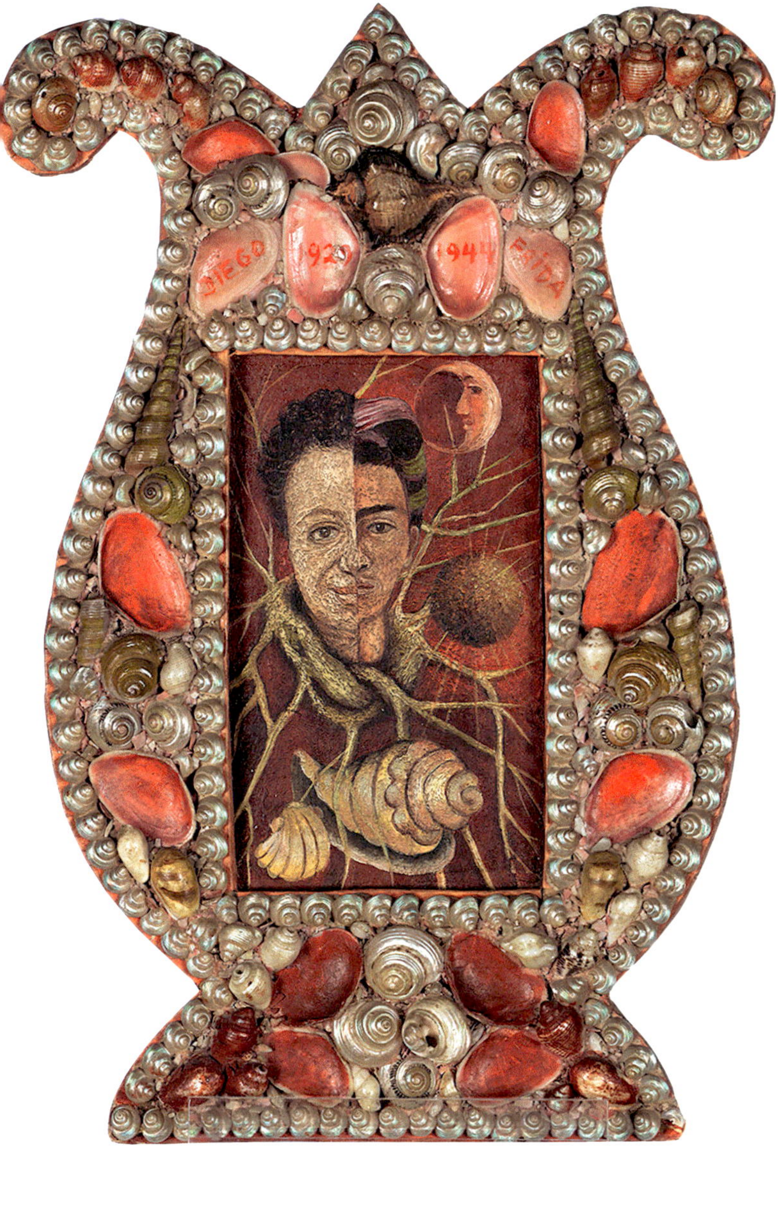


16 *Diego and Frida, 1929–1944,* 1944, oil on hardboard, 12.3 × 7.4 cm, Private collection

to New York. Back in Mexico, she met and fell in love with the sculptor Isamu Noguchi. In the period that followed, her productivity reached a new peak.

Frida Kahlo and Diego Rivera divorced in September 1939. They remarried on December 8 of the following year, but agreed on mutual independence. In 1943, Kahlo painted two pictures in which she placed Rivera in the seeing center of her forehead as the focus of her thoughts (15). In 1944, for their fifteenth wedding anniversary, she merged herself and her partner in the double face of *Diego and Frida, 1929–1944* (16)—fundamentally different and yet inseparable.

## PAINTING: A LIBERATION FROM SUFFERING

From around 1929 on, Kahlo began to paint freely, self-confidently developing her own style. Even before her first solo exhibition in New York in 1938, she succeeded in selling several paintings. Kahlo announced tongue-in-cheek to the Detroit News that Rivera, "the young lad," was doing his thing "quite well, of course, but the really great artist is me."[14]



But what makes her a great artist? Time and again people have questioned whether Frida Kahlo's work would have triumphed without the link to her eventful biography. But it is precisely in the "inseparable unity of the human and the artistic"[15] that the fascination lies. Kahlo's feelings of otherness and inadequacy, which made her look for faults and weaknesses in herself, then the defiant, self-suggestive response in transforming her needs and neediness into toughness and strength, as well as the unbroken effort to endure her sufferings, were part of her contradictory nature. In her imperfection lay her humanity. Her warmth, empathy, immediacy, and passion made her likeable. "This woman's personality was so complex and contradictory that one could say there were many Fridas," Alejandro Gómez Arias recalled of his childhood friend, "perhaps none was the person she wanted to be."[16]

Following a cultural impulse of the revolution, Kahlo adapted the rich folk art of her homeland. If nothing else, the independent Tehuana has since been an idol for a new, liberated Mexico. When André Breton came to Mexico in 1938 on behalf of the French Foreign Ministry, he enthusiastically appropriated Kahlo as a Surrealist: her painting was

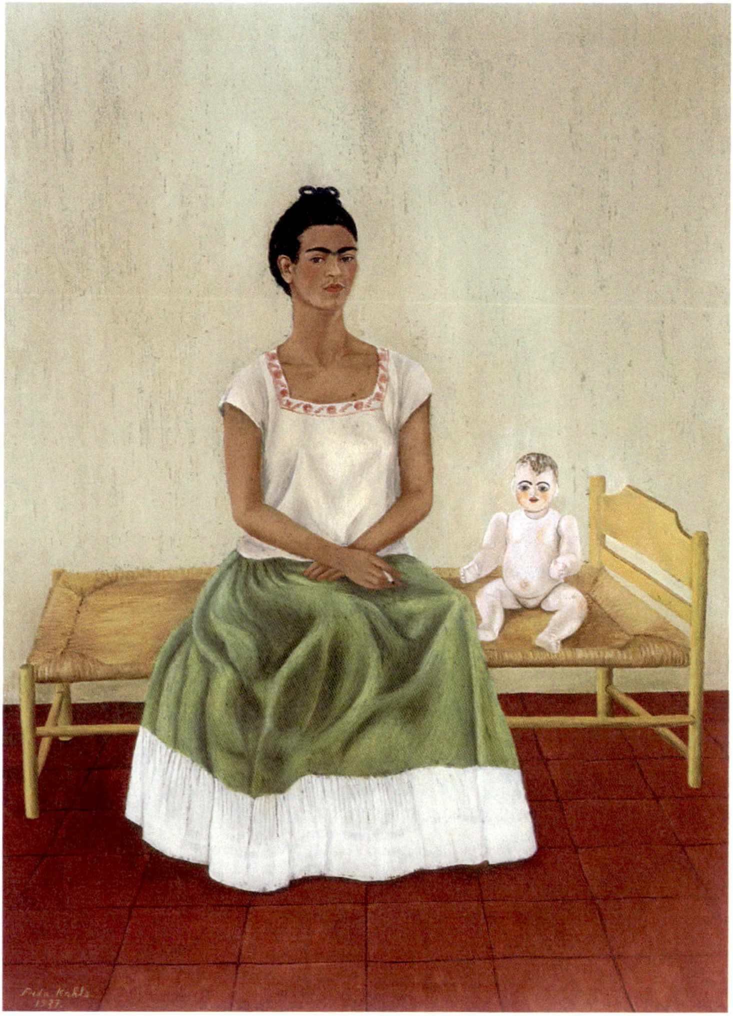

17 *Me and My Doll,* 1937, oil on metal, 40 × 31 cm
Jacques and Natasha Gelman Collection, Mexico City

"like a ribbon wrapped around a bomb."[17] Moreover, the feminism of the Surrealist art movement, which was dominated by men, found its ideal in Kahlo's individuality. But as she emphasized: "I never painted dreams. I painted my own reality."[18] How blurred this difference can be is shown in the painting *What the Water Gave Me* (18), painted in the same year, which illustrates both real and surreal stations of her life to date. Still, what guided Kahlo was not a conscious rebellion against convention or an emphasis on the irrational. "I really do not know if my paintings are surrealistic or not, but what I do know is that I express myself in them without ever giving a damn about the judgments or prejudices of others."[19]

Kahlo, who endured more than thirty operations in her life, felt anything but free. In her art she was allowed to be so; here she reflected reality and desire, but also hardship and bitterness. Her openness was unsparing, for example in the small picture with the sarcastic title *A Few Small Nips*. Its cruel bloodbath, responding to Rivera's affair with Cristina after a year without taking up a paintbrush, spills over onto the frame, bursting the painterly illusion of the canvas and entering the reality of the viewer. But what in Kahlo's works seems mysterious, at times also frightening, even chilling, becomes comprehensible against the background of her biography.

In this context, the self-portrait *The Broken Column* from 1944 stands out. Kahlo painted it in the double sense of the word after an operation on her spine, the corset once again depriving her of freedom. The damaged architectural supporting structure in the center of her open, nail-strewn torso symbolizes both support and destruction. Kahlo, meanwhile, accepts this fate without expression. Two years later, while she was undergoing a painful bone transplantation on her spine in New York, which bound her to the sickbed for many months, she produced *Tree of Hope* (4) and *The Wounded Deer* (19). In it her wounds are evident: two deep cuts, nine bloody arrows. But feelings of confidence, drawn from nature, from the Aztec creation with which she feels deeply connected as "*La Mexicana*," are also evident.

In 1949 Frida Kahlo made an attempt to end her life; in 1950 she found hope and again underwent a complicated operation. But because the wound under the hardened plaster repeatedly became infected, she remained in the American Hospital in Mexico City for a whole year and

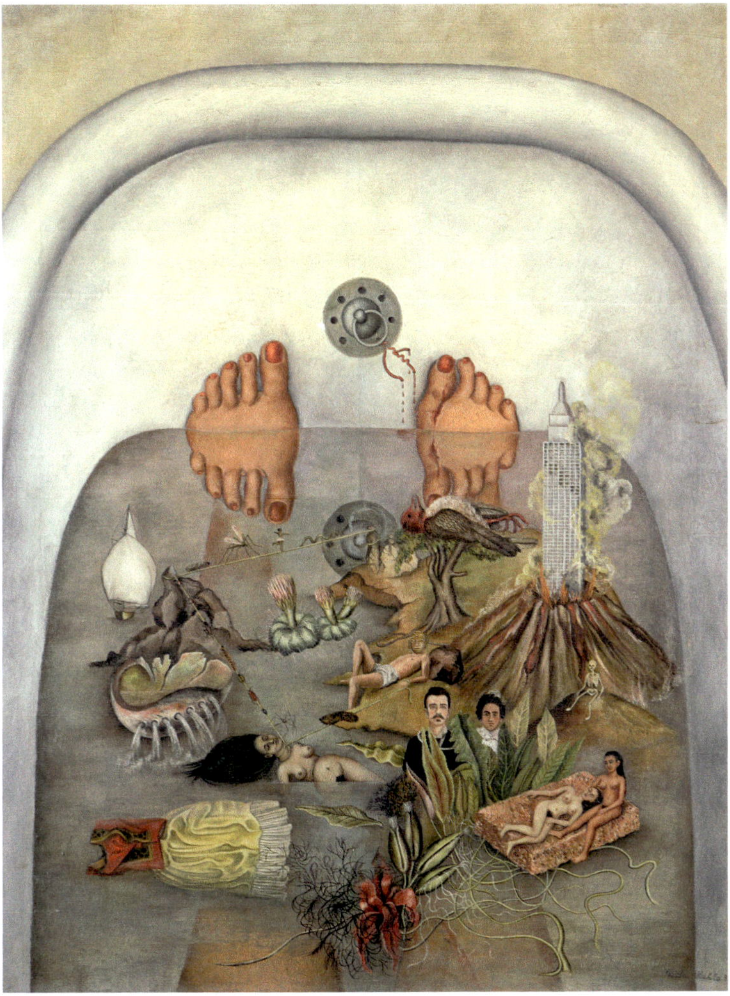

**18** *What the Water Gave Me (What I Saw in the Water),* 1938
Oil on canvas, 91 × 70.5 cm, Private collection

Following double page:
**19** *The Wounded Deer,* 1946, oil on Masonite, 22.4 × 30 cm, Private collection

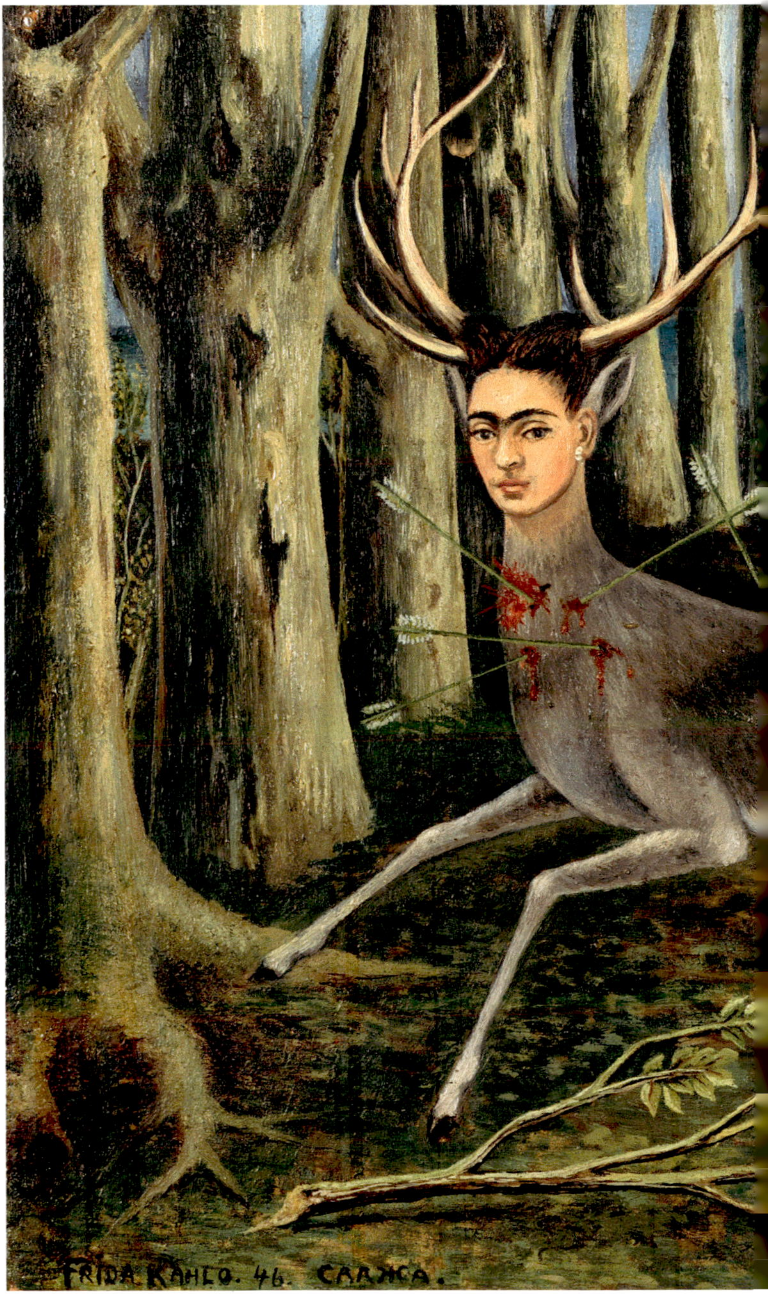
FRIDA KAHLO. 46.

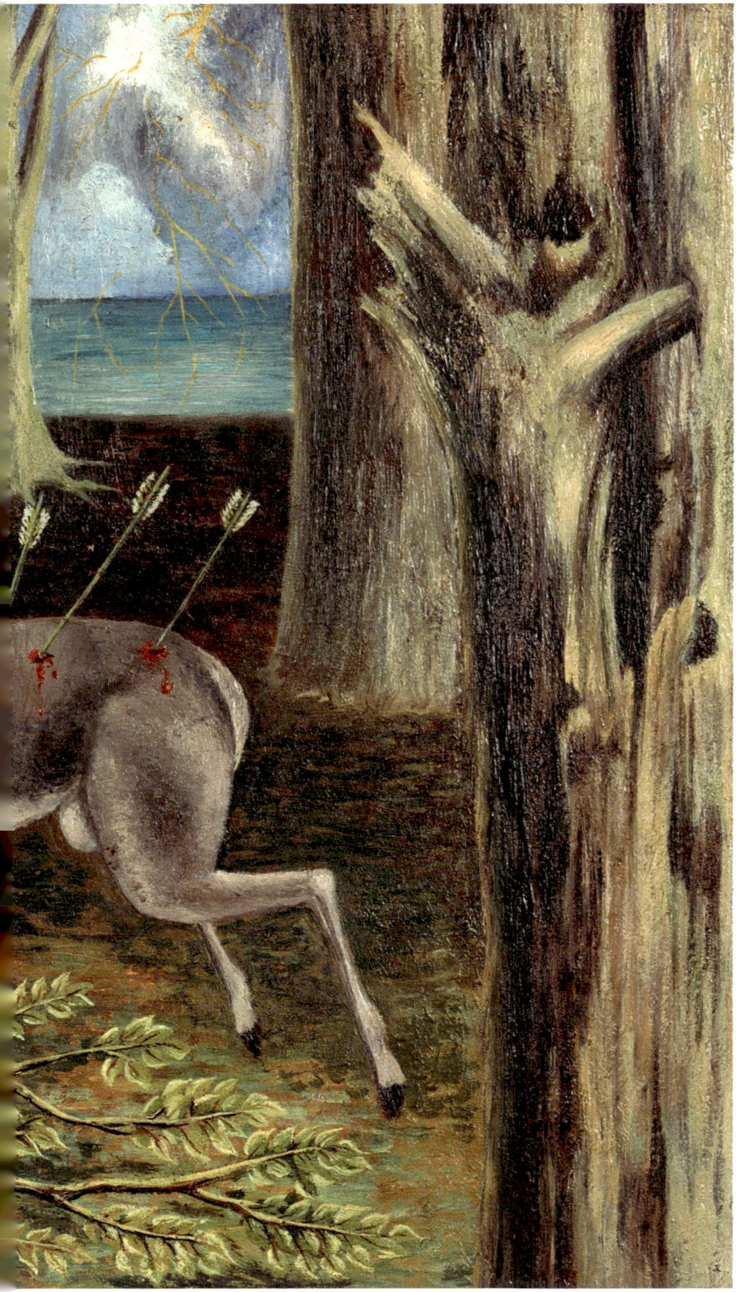

for six more operations. To her visitors, meanwhile, she appeared eternally vivacious and optimistic, surrounding herself with things that reminded her of her well-being at home, her room decorated with photographs, sugar skulls, and Judas figures. Watching movies and performing little puppet shows, with Cristina's help, Kahlo dressed up as if she were going out, playacting normalcy. In a self-prescribed euphemism, brought on by high doses of morphine, she painted over her illness with the help of a pocket mirror, cotton swabs, and tinctures of iodine, as well as brushes and her own paints: the plaster corsets now bore flowers, fruit, hammer, and sickle. Back in the Blue House, henceforth in a wheelchair, she felt "a despair that no words can describe. Nevertheless, I feel like living."[20]

In the subsequent period she painted above all still lifes (21). They too reveal Kahlo's innermost being under the sun and the moon, between suffering and love, man and woman. More than ever she turned to politics, wanted to live for the revolution.[21] Under the influence of painkillers, her brushstrokes became increasingly rough and erratic as she painted in



**20** *Sun and Life*, 1947, oil on Masonite, 40 × 50 cm, Private collection

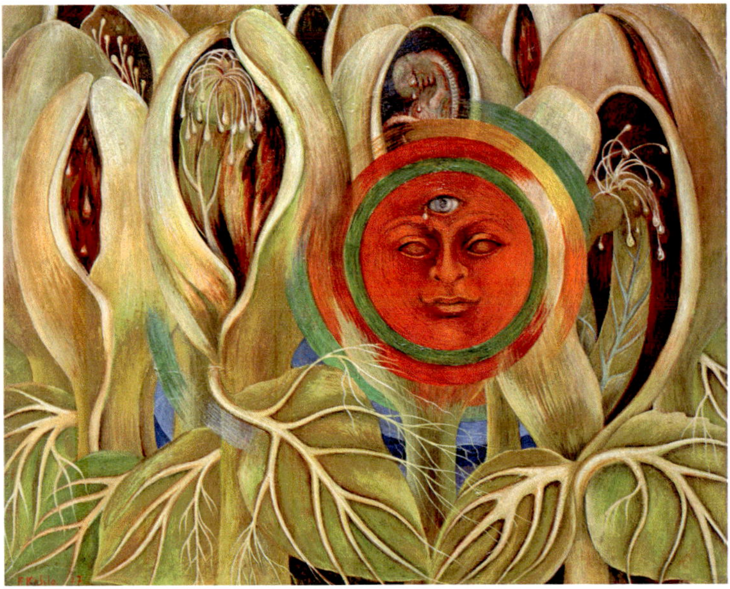

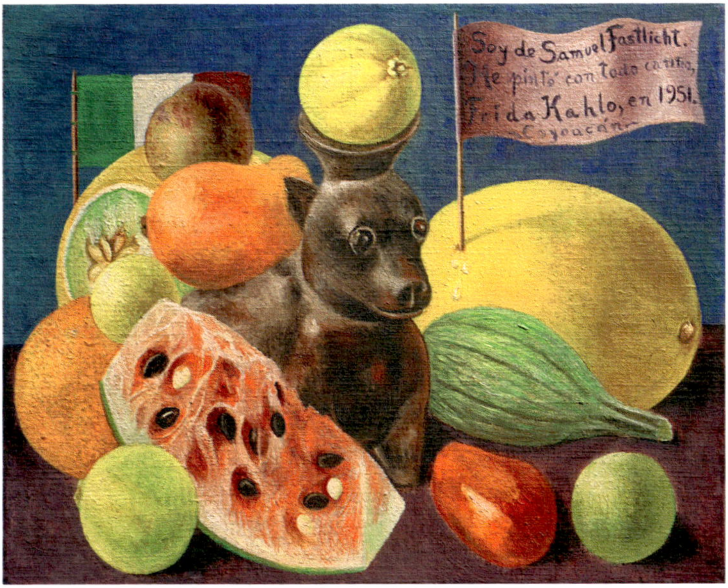


**21** *Still Life (Dedicated to Samuel Fastlicht)*, 1951, oil on Masonite, 28.6 × 35.9 cm, Private collection

fantasy and in the desire for death. Her last picture from 1954 is titled *Viva la vida*—Long Live Life (22).

## A LIFE FOR THE ARTS: EMANCIPATION AND SUCCESS

Kahlo's imagination captured ever more complex worlds on paper, canvas, and metal. Creating images in order to live, her depicted gaze looks almost imperceptibly past the viewer; often it is her companions, such as the little monkeys, or the tame deer Granizo and her niece Isolda in *The Wounded Table*, who—reflecting the gleam of Kahlo's eyes—vicariously make direct eye contact.

"My paintings are carefully painted, not with ease, but with patience."[22] With the meticulousness of the tiniest brushstrokes, Kahlo began the laborious work in the upper left corner. "She seemed to be painting out an image that already existed in her imagination."[23] Fine, dense hairs on Kahlo's cheeks, for example, were repeated in the fur of a monkey and in the floral

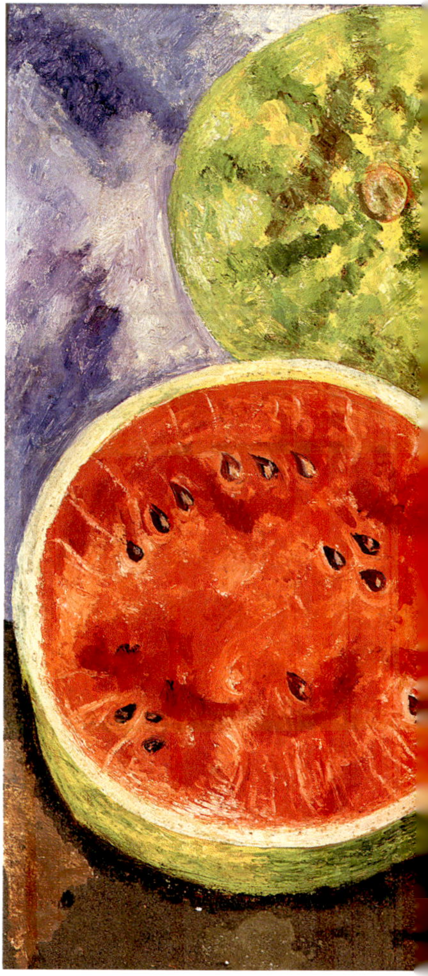

**22** *Viva la vida,* 1954, oil on hardboard, 59.5 × 50.8 cm
Museo Frida Kahlo, Mexico City

fluff of the undersides of leaves. Everything became a significant detail. Everything arose from direct, truthful, existential experience, understanding, and feeling of its creator. Kahlo creates her own reality, which is at once revelation and suppression, self-knowledge and self-concealment.

Kahlo's first solo exhibition took place at Julien Levy's New York gallery from November 1 to 5, 1938, with all twenty-five works created up to

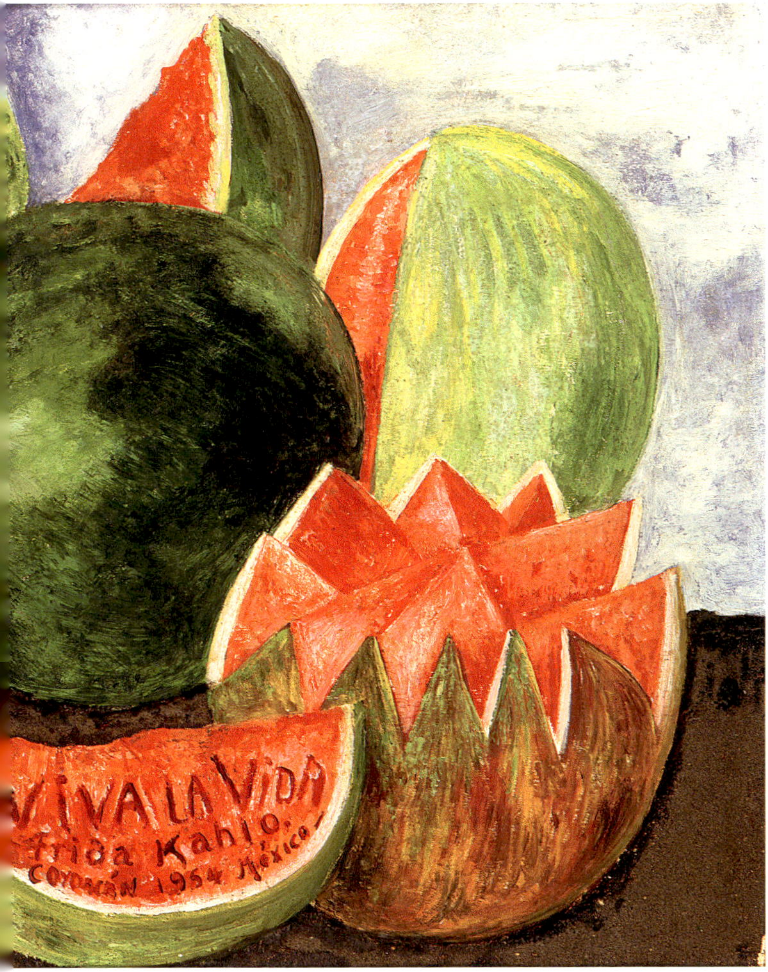


then. Diego Rivera wrote the critic Sam A. Lewisohn: “I recommend this artist to you, not as a husband, but as an enthusiastic admirer of her work, caustic and tender, hard as steel and delicate and fine as a butterfly’s wing, admirable as a beautiful smile and profound and cruel as the bitterness of life.”[24] After the show, Frida Kahlo finally made the leap from Rivera’s shadow to artistic autonomy and recognition, as well as

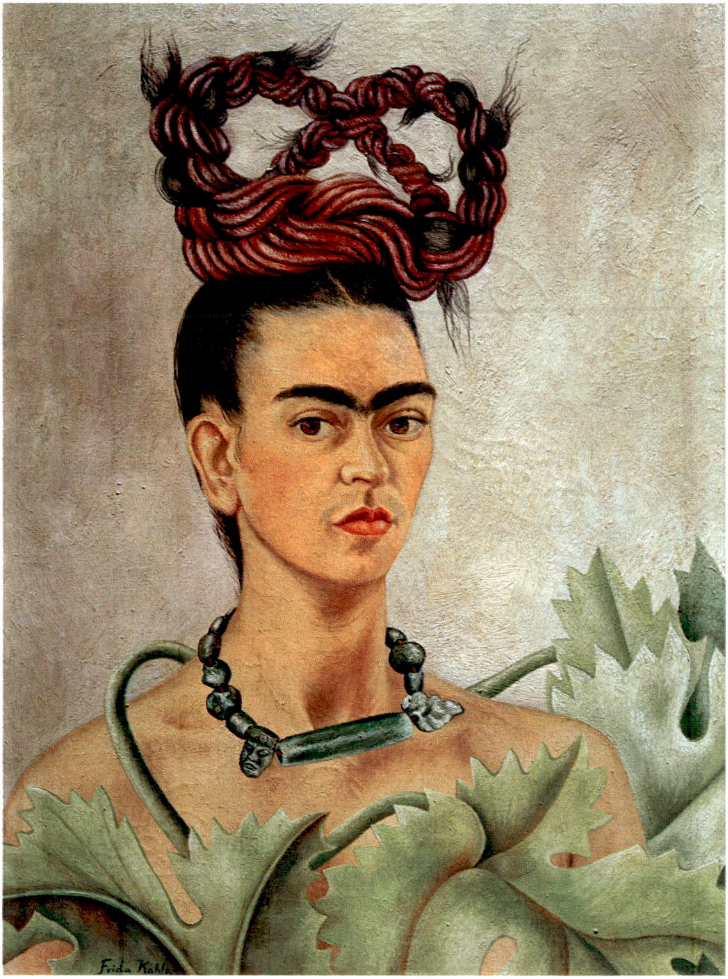


**23** *Self-Portrait with Braid,* 1941, oil on hardboard, 51 × 38.5 cm, Jacques and Natasha Gelman Collection, Mexico City

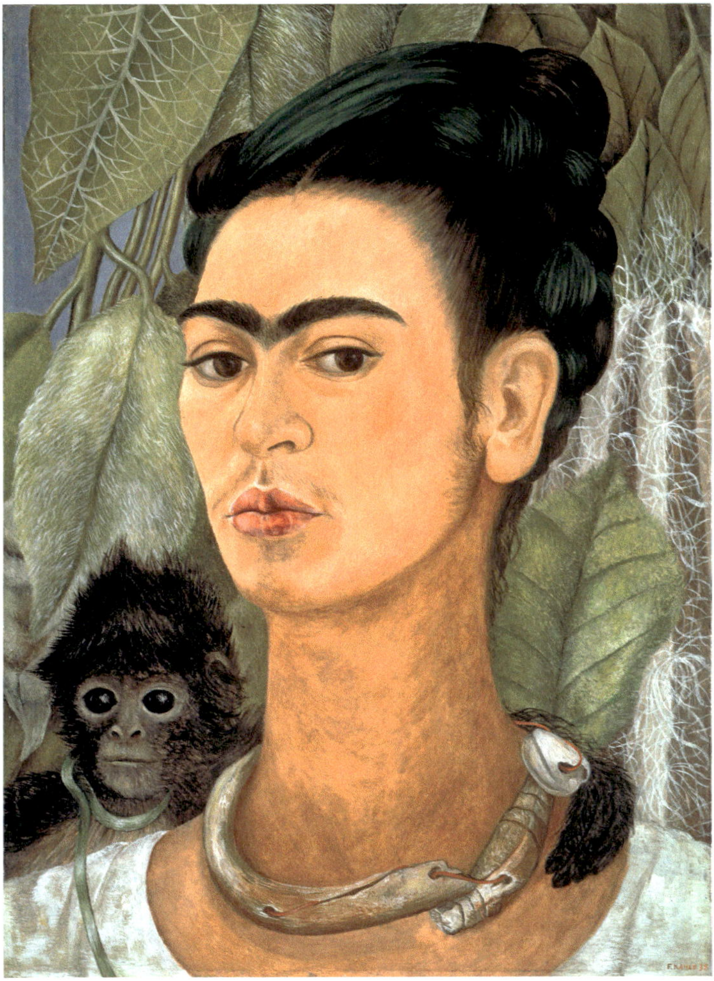

**24** *Self-Portrait with Monkey,* 1938, oil on hardboard, 40.6 × 30.5 cm
Albright-Knox Art Gallery, Buffalo, New York

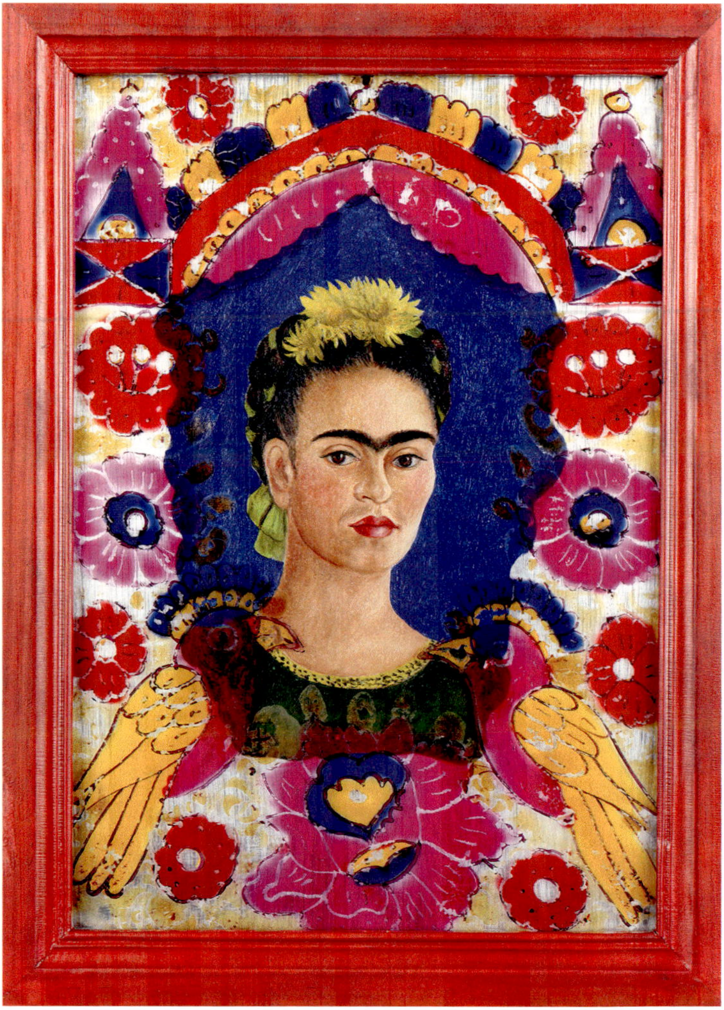

**25** *The Frame (Self-Portrait),* c. 1938, oil on glass, 60 × 80 cm, Musée National d'Art Moderne, Centre Pompidou, Paris

financial independence. Half of her paintings were sold and more sales were imminent.

She kept her love affairs—with men as well as women—secret; a brief relationship with Leon Trotsky taught her Rivera's jealousy. Kahlo enjoyed Julien Levy's attention and soon after began an intense liaison with Nickolas Muray, a well-known pioneer of color photography. Once again, Kahlo became the coveted object of a camera—and seemed to feel comfortable doing so. At this turning point, soon to be the high point of her career, her self-dramatization achieved perfection. The positive response from the outside world reflected her own ideal of an emancipated and committed, popular and beloved artist and woman.

In early 1939 André Breton endeavored to pave the way for her to exhibit in Paris. But the only positive thing Kahlo found in France was the painter Marcel Duchamp's commitment to her art. Seventeen of her paintings were eventually shown at the Renou & Colle gallery; her admirers included Joan Miró, Wassily Kandinsky, Yves Tanguy, Wolfgang Paalen, and Pablo Picasso, who gave Kahlo a pair of earrings in the shape of hands. The Louvre acquired the colorful self-portrait *The Frame* (25). Kahlo's own hands, covered in the jewelry of Mexican heritage and fashionable modernism, appeared on the cover of *Vogue*.

Nevertheless, she did not want to stay in a Europe overshadowed by the fear of war. Since 1935 Kahlo had written her first name "Frieda" without the German "e". She now turned down an offer from Peggy Guggenheim's gallery in London. Other cultural figures and intellectuals, including Sergei Eisenstein, Leonora Carrington, Henri Cartier-Bresson, and Josef and Anni Albers, were similarly drawn to Mexico. They fled into exile to escape the intensifying Fascism; at the same time, they were attracted by Mexico's abundance of nature and folk traditions.

Inés Amor's Galería de Arte Mexicano in Mexico City inaugurated the "International Surrealist Exhibition" on January 17, 1940. Kahlo contributed her only two large-format pictures: the double portrait *The Two Fridas* (3) and the now lost oil painting *The Wounded Table* (38) from 1939/40. The latter assembled, as if on a theater stage, many of the elements that stood for aspects of her self-reflection in her œuvre in a kind of Last Supper scene (Kahlo painted the picture at the age of 33). Depicted are a pre-Columbian clay statue (*ídolo*) from Rivera's collection of 10,000 pieces, representing ancient Mexico; the body of a Judas figure

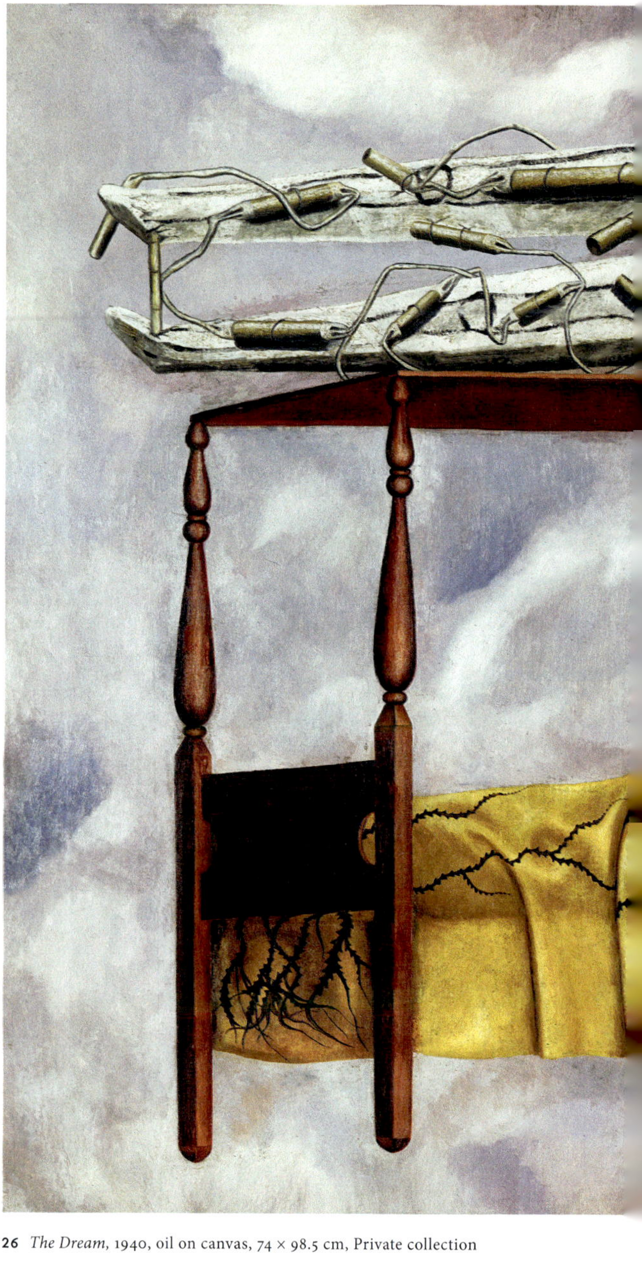

**26** *The Dream,* 1940, oil on canvas, 74 × 98.5 cm, Private collection

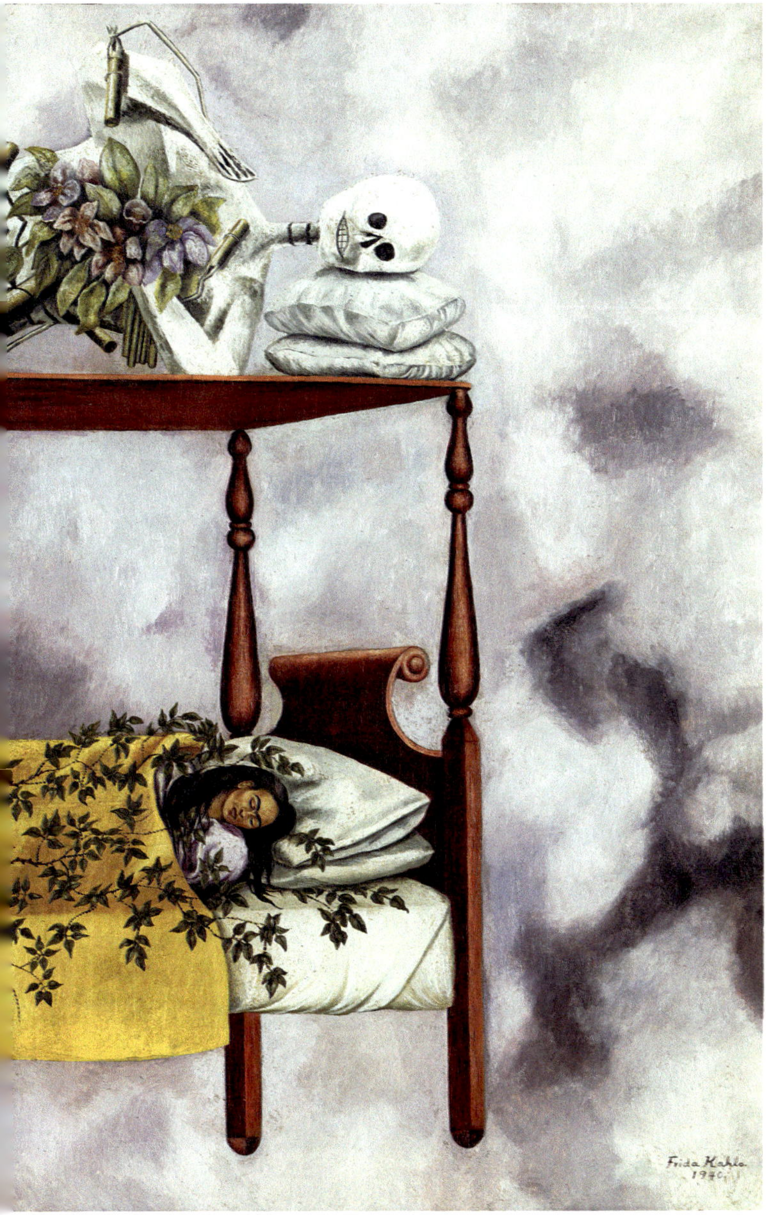
Frida Kahlo
1940

peppered with fireworks, reflecting the custom of exorcizing evil; a skeleton as a reminder of ever-present death; the wounded right feet in almost all those depicted; and bleeding wounds in the body of the table. In the same year, the *Self-Portrait with Thorn Necklace* (27) similarly drew a parallel to Christian martyrdom. In her other bust portraits, red silk ribbons, floral tendrils, veins, chains, or the arms of a spider monkey wrap themselves meaningfully around the neck of the Woman of Sorrows, who can now call herself Latin America's most famous woman artist.

A positive turning point in 1943 was Kahlo's teaching activity for the anti-authoritarian painting and sculpture school La Esmeralda, which opened in 1942. Due to her physical limitations, she soon moved it from the city to the Blue House; her seven students were enthusiastic and faithfully called themselves "Los Fridos." Together they revived the popular folk tradition of the mural paintings in the *pulquería* taverns.

In 1947, only four women artists were represented in the show "Forty-Five Self-Portraits by Mexican Painters from the Eighteenth to the Twentieth Century" at the Palacio de Bellas Artes; Kahlo was one of them with her *Self-Portrait as Tehuana* (15). Two years later she participated in the opening of the Mexican Salon of Fine Arts with *The Love Embrace of the Universe, the Earth (Mexico), Myself, Diego, and Señor Xólotl* (p. 8).



Kahlo experienced her first solo show in Mexico in the spring of 1953. Since her state of health was critical, she spontaneously became the central display object of the exhibition: the artist as enthroned on her richly decorated canopy bed in the center of the Galería de Arte Contemporáneo. While admirers stood in line before the bed, perhaps the same persons who only a year later would be offering their condolences before her coffin, a mirror fixed to the canopy allowed her integration into the event. The exhibition was a tremendous success.

## UNMASKED: THE DIARY AS MIRROR OF THE INTERIOR

The contrast to the conceptual openness of her paintings created for the public is found in the intimacy of Kahlo's associatively painted diary. She began it between 1942 and 1944 after her father's death, filling it with

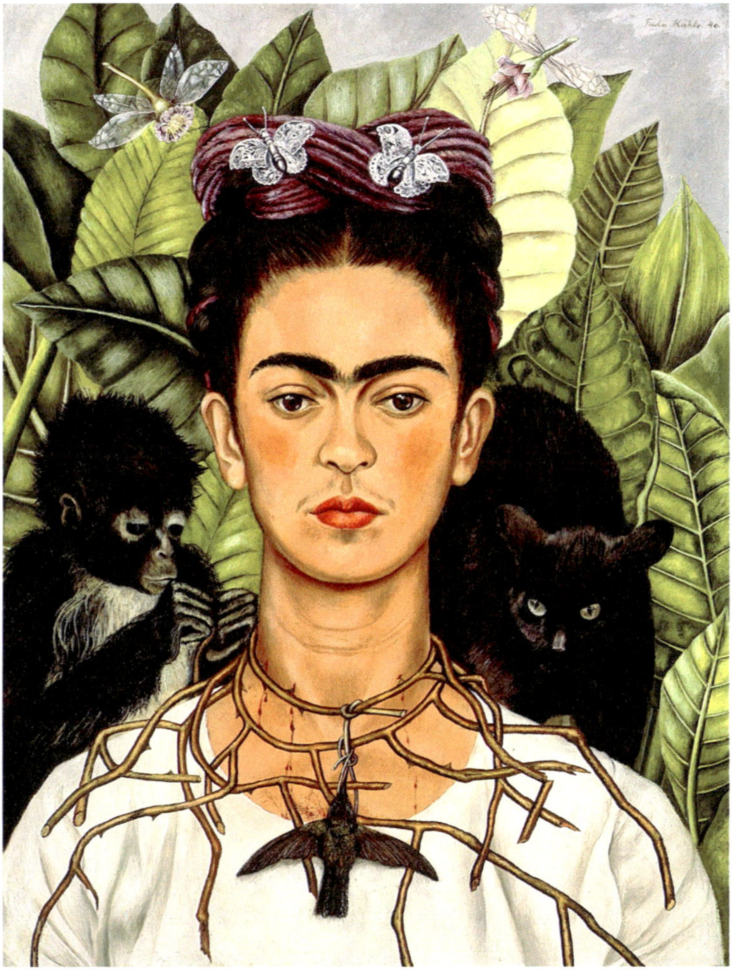

27 *Self-Portrait with Thorn Necklace,* 1940, oil on canvas, 61.3 × 47 cm,
Harry Ransom Center, University of Texas at Austin

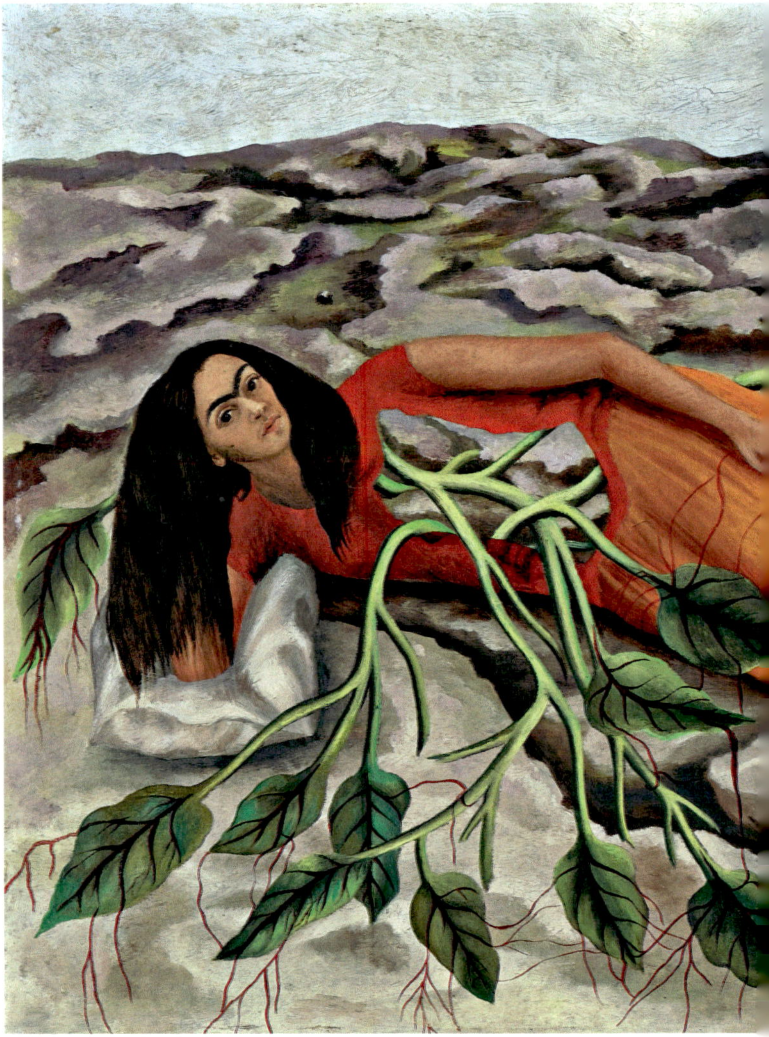

**28** *Roots,* 1943, oil on canvas, 30 × 50.3 cm, Private collection

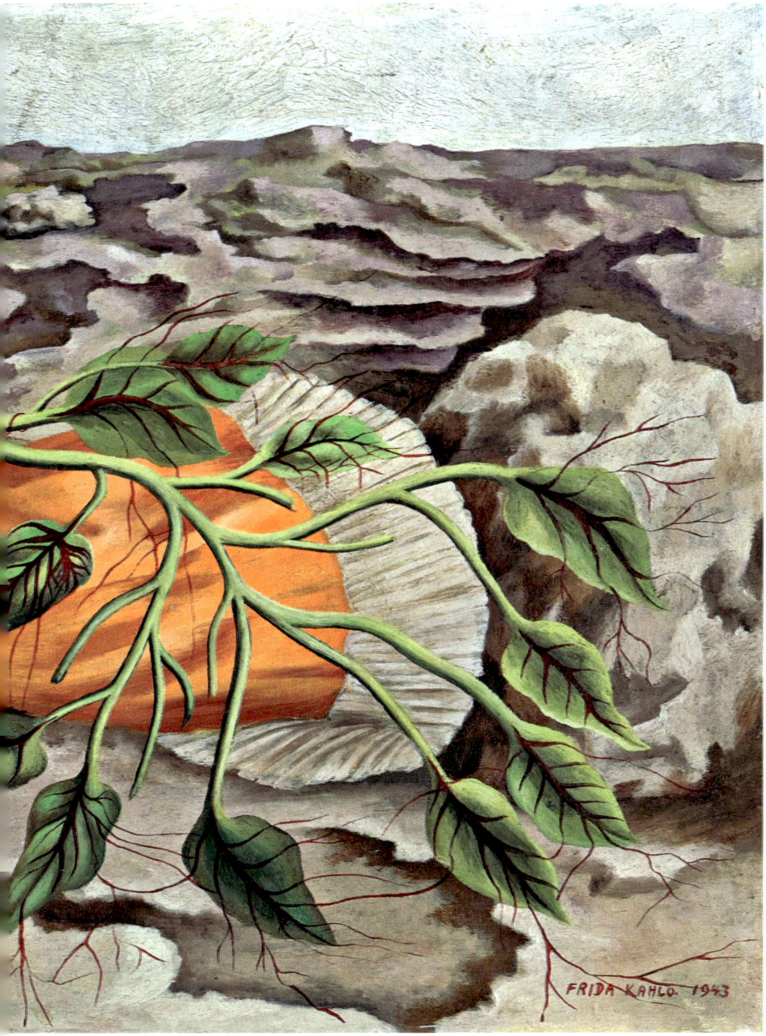
FRIDA KAHLO. 1943

sketches in which one form evokes the next, a process termed "automatic drawing" by the Surrealists: vividly flowing word and thought games on life, death, illness, fear, on human diversity or Mexican heritage; messages of love to Diego; inkblots that immediately develop into fictional faces or animals; a six-page autobiography; dedications to artistic models such as Hieronymus Bosch and detailed thoughts on communism; the intuitive attribution of the colors she used to moods and emotions; recipes for pigment mixtures; and, shortly before her death, with long lists of thanks to her friends, doctors, companions, and to the strong side of herself. "I thank myself and my enormous will to live with all those who love me and for all those I love."[25] In her diary, Kahlo allowed herself to love—and suffer—completely unmasked.

"Nothing is more important than laughter," Kahlo notes.[26] But in August 1953, her *alegría*, the positive, strong self-image she maintained with all her might, was ultimately crushed. Numerous drawn diary entries deal with the amputation of her lower right leg; the gangrene attacking her foot could no longer be stopped. She was operated on, received a prosthesis, painted *My Family* (29) lying down with the help of a special easel, and in



**29** *My Family, 1950–1954,* oil on hardboard, 41 × 59 cm, Museo Frida Kahlo, Mexico City

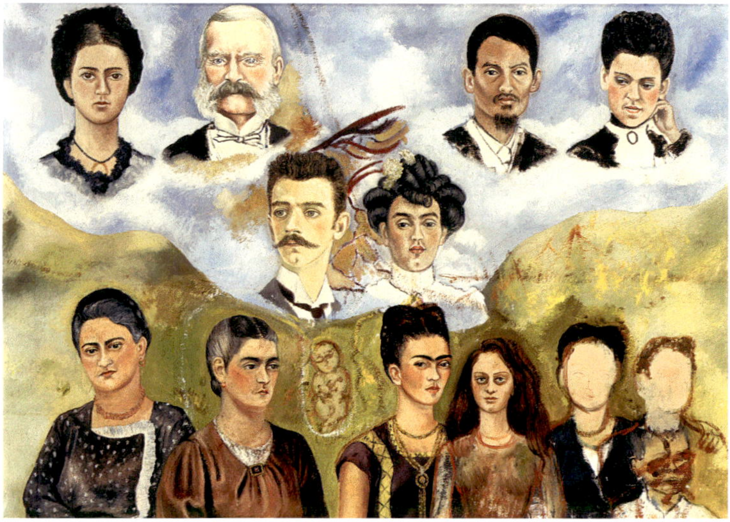

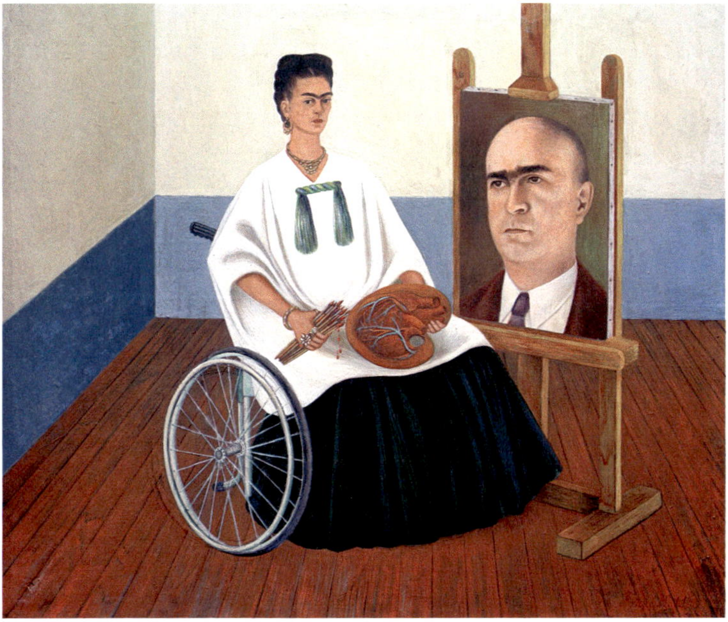

**30** *Self-Portrait with Portrait of Dr. Farill,* 1951, oil on hardboard, 41.5 × 50 cm, Private collection

a plaster corset created the *Self-Portrait with Portrait of Dr. Farill* (30), the doctor in whose care she had last put herself. Psychologically, however, she would not recover from this intervention, which for her was an aggression, because it took away a part of herself.

The symbol of wings appears repeatedly in her private diary entries. "Feet, what do I need you for when I have wings to fly with," she states poetically, continuing "Yo soy la DESINTEGRACIÓN," I am disintegration. Kahlo sketches herself as an angel, burning in blazing flames. "Te vas? No. ALAS ROTAS" (Are you going? No. Broken wings), she comments on the stagnation she sadly perceives. She takes leave of the world with lightness: "I happily await leaving the house—and hope never to come back—FRIDA."[27] Her last drawn entry is a black angel of death.

It is not definitively known whether she committed suicide on July 13, 1954, at the age of forty-seven. Officially the cause of death was a pulmonary embolism. After her death most of her pictures were sold or given away. In July 1958 the Frida Kahlo Museum was inaugurated in the Blue House. Her personal estate was first discovered in 2004 and made public in 2007; it includes 22,000 documents, over 6,000 photographs, and almost 300 personal objects. In 1977 the Mexican government commemorated the artist with a retrospective, declaring in 1984 Frida Kahlo's entire œuvre a national monument.

---

**TERESA GRENZMANN** *works as a journalist, author, and editor in Munich. She studied journalism, art history, and theatre studies. Since 2004 she has written for the arts section of the* Frankfurter Allgemeine Zeitung, *among others.*



1 From an interview between Hayden Herrera and Antonio Rodriguez, August 1977, Mexico City, quoted in: Hayden Herrera, *Frida Kahlo. Die Gemälde* (Munich: 1992), p. 7.
2 Cf. Sarah M. Lowe (ed.), *Gemaltes Tagebuch*, (Munich: 1995), p. 247.
3 Herrera 1992 (see note 1), p. 12.
4 Salomon Grimberg, "Fridas Freunde sind auch meine Freunde. Oder: Wer sammelt Kunst von Frida Kahlo," in: Helga Prignitz-Poda and Peter von Becker (eds.), *Frida Kahlo, Retrospektive*, exh. cat. Martin-Gropius-Bau, Berlin; Bank Austria Forum, Vienna, 2010 (Munich, et al.: 2010), p. 29.
5 Raquel Tibol, *Frida Kahlo—Ein offenes Leben* (Munich: 2005), p. 50.
6 Frida Kahlo in an interview with Raquel Tibol; see Tibol 2005 (see note 5), p. 51.
7 Herrera 1992 (see note 1), p. 30.
8 Hayden Herrera, *Frida Kahlo. Ein leidenschaftliches Leben* (Frankfurt am Main: 2008), p. 311.
9 Tibol 2005 (see note 5), p. 197.
10 Frida Kahlo 1947 in the catalogue for the exhibition "Forty-Five Self-Portraits by Mexican Painters from the Eighteenth to the Twentieth Centuries" at the Palacio de Bellas Artes; quoted in Tibol 2005 (see note 5), p. 9.
11 Dolores Álvarez Bravo in an interview with Hayden Herrera, September 1974, Mexico City, in Herrera 1992 (see note 1), p. 11.
12 Lowe 1995 (see note 2), p. 254.
13 Ibid., p. 270.
14 Quoted in Herrera 2008 (see note 8), p. 142.
15 Tibol 2005 (see note 5), p. 136.
16 "Un testimonio sobre Frida Kahlo," in *Frida Kahlo, Tina Modotti*. exh. cat. Museo Nacional de Arte (Mexico City: 1983), p. 79.
17 "La peinture de Frida Kahlo de Rivera est un ruban autour d'une bombe." André Breton in his foreword "Frida Kahlo de Rivera" for the catalogue of the exhibition in the Julien Levy Gallery. Quoted in Elena Poniatowska, Carla Stellweg, Carole Kismaric, *Die verführte Kamera. Ein photographisches Porträt von Frida Kahlo* (Basel: 1992), p. 113.
18 *Time*, April 27, 1953, p. 90; quoted in Lowe 1995 (see note 2), p. 287 and Herrera 1992 (see note 1), p. 72.
19 Frida Kahlo 1947 in the catalogue for the exhibition "Forty-Five Self-Portraits by Mexican Painters from the Eighteenth to the Twentieth Centuries" at the Palacio de Bellas Artes; quoted in Tibol 2005 (see note 5), p. 148.

20 Lowe 1995 (see note 2), p. 252.

21 "I have to fight with all my strength so that the small positive things my health allows me to say can help the revolution. The only reason to live." Quoted in Lowe 1995 (see note 2), p. 252.

22 Tibol 2005 (see note 5), p. 85.

23 Herrera 1992 (see note 1), p. 17.

24 Tibol 2005 (see note 5), p. 88.

25 Lowe 1995 (see note 2), p. 279ff.

26 Ibid., p. 239.

27 Ibid., pp. 252, 269, 274, 276ff., 285.

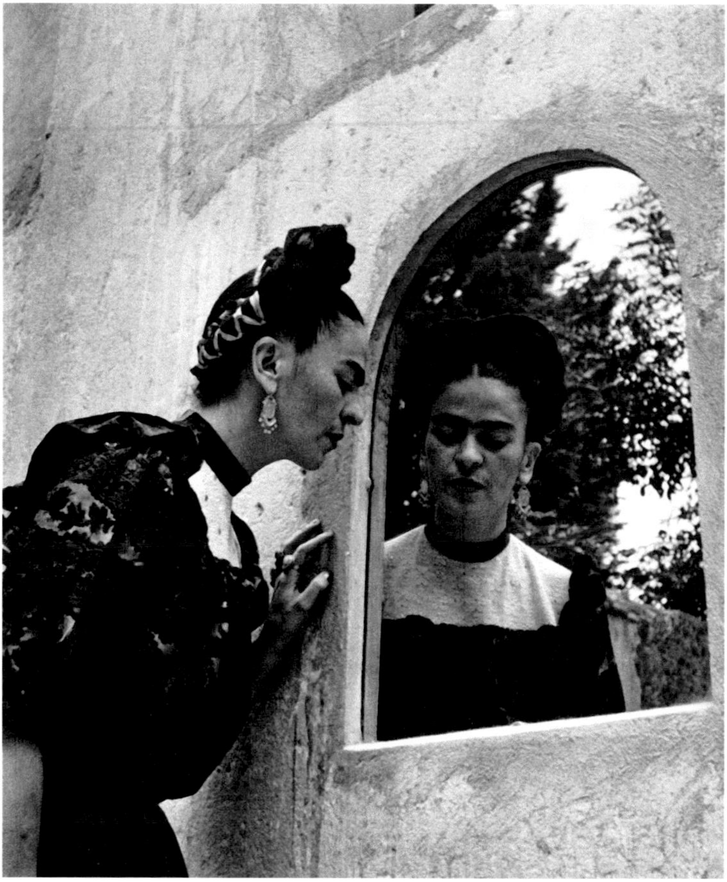

**31** Frida Kahlo, 1944

# BIOGRAPHY

Frida Kahlo

1907–1954

**1907** Magdalena Carmen Frieda Kahlo y Calderón is born on July 6 in the "Casa Azul" (Blue House) in Coyoacán, Mexico, the daughter of Guillermo Kahlo and Matilde Calderón y Gonzales. Due to a defect of the spinal column (spina bifida), presumably congenital, she suffers from afflictions in her right leg and foot from childhood.

**1910** In September the Mexican Revolution breaks out, triggered by an uprising after the celebrations for the hundredth anniversary of independence. Kahlo later claims that she was born in 1910.

**1922** Kahlo is accepted into the Escuela Nacional Preparatoria in Mexico City prior to beginning medical studies. She joins the "Cachuchas" and falls in love with its leader, Alejandro Gómez Arias. Her first encounter with the famous painter Diego Rivera takes place during this year.

**1925** Kahlo takes lessons at the etching workshop of the graphic artist Fernando Fernández. Now aged eighteen, she is severely injured during a traffic accident in Mexico City on September 17. A tram crashes into the bus she is riding and a metal holding rod impales her from shoulder to abdomen. She suffers several fractures and severe injuries. After this traumatic experience she decides to become a painter, incorporating the blow of fate into her œuvre.

**1926** Kahlo creates her first painted *Self-Portrait in Velvet Dress* (5), which she dedicates to Alejandro Gómez Arias.

**1928** Frida Kahlo joins the Communist Party.

**1929** On August 21, Frida Kahlo and Diego Rivera, twenty years her senior, are married. Kahlo is his third wife. She paints the self-portrait *Time Flies*. Rivera is expelled from the Communist Party.

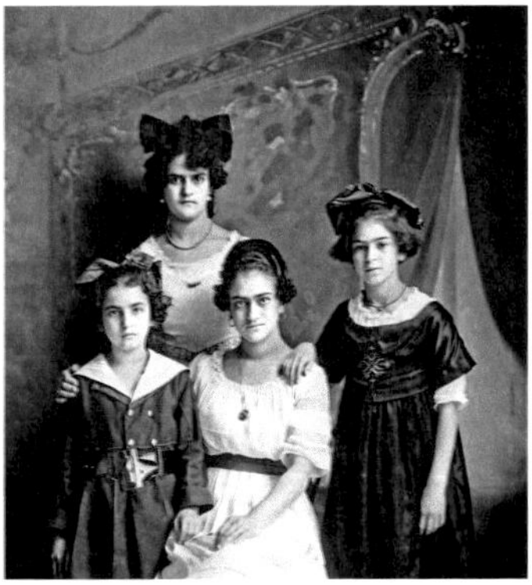

**32** Frida Kahlo (right) with her sisters Cristina, and Adriana, and her mother Matilde, photographed by their father, 1916

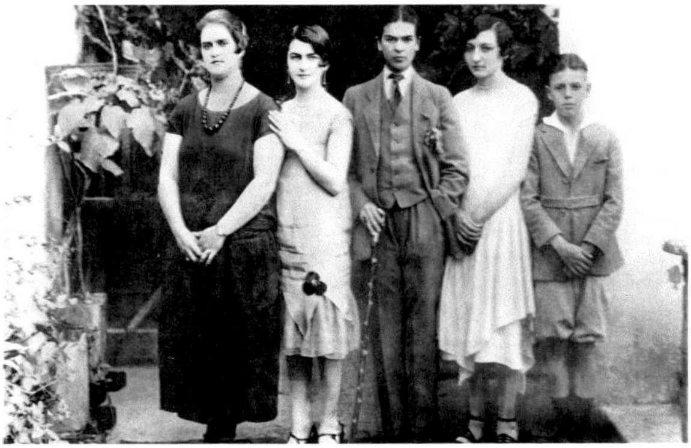

**33** Frida Kahlo in man's suit (center) with her mother Mathilde, sister Cristina, and two other relatives, 1926

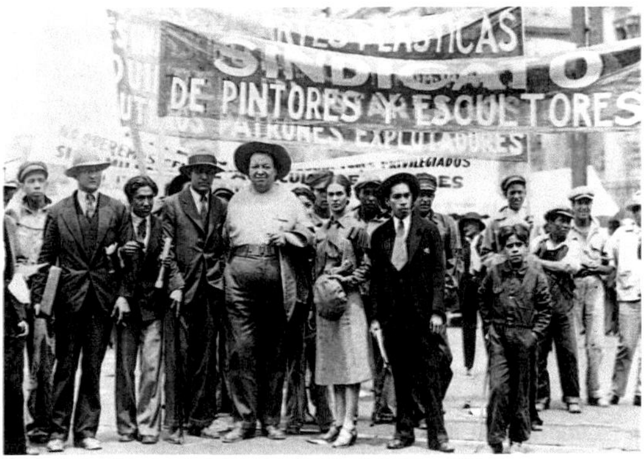


**34** Diego Rivera and Frida Kahlo at a demonstration on May 1 in Mexico City, 1929

**1930–1933** Kahlo accompanies Rivera on his trip to fulfil commissions in San Francisco, Detroit, and New York. She meets the photographers Edward Weston and Imogen Cunningham, as well as the physician Leo Eloesser, with whom she will maintain a lifelong friendship. In 1930 she suffers the first of several miscarriages as a result of a failed abortion. Further works are created, including the wedding picture *Frida and Diego Rivera* (13), which is shown at the "Sixth Annual Exhibition of the San Francisco Society of Women Artists." In 1932, she has another miscarriage in Detroit, which she addresses in the paintings *Henry Ford Hospital, Frida and the Miscarriage* (10), and *My Birth*. On September 15 Kahlo's mother dies. She critically regards the United States in her *Self-Portrait on the Borderline Between Mexico and the United States* (12) and *My Dress Hangs There* (11). After returning to Mexico in December 1933, Kahlo and Rivera move into their new duplex in San Angel.

**1934** Kahlo suffers another miscarriage. Rivera has an affair with Frida Kahlo's younger sister Cristina.



**1935** Frida Kahlo sarcastically expresses her disappointment over Rivera's affair in the painting *A Few Small Nips*. She travels alone to New York. Back in Mexico, she meets and falls in love with the sculptor Isamu Noguchi. Kahlo begins to paint her family tree, *My Grandparents, My Parents, and Me*.

**1937** Leon Trotsky and his wife Natalia arrive in Mexico City during their exile. They live in the Blue House and a brief love affair develops between Kahlo and the Russian revolutionary. Kahlo participates in a group exhibition at the art gallery of the Universidad Autónoma in Mexico City. She creates the paintings *My Nurse and I*, *Fulang Chang and I* (2), *Memory*, and *Me and My Doll* (17).

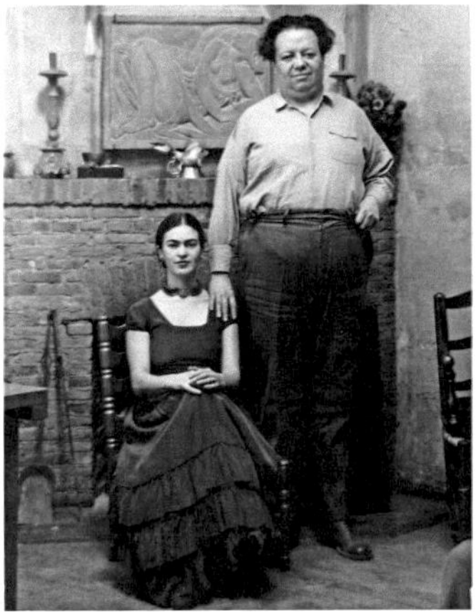

**35** Frida Kahlo and Diego Rivera, 1931

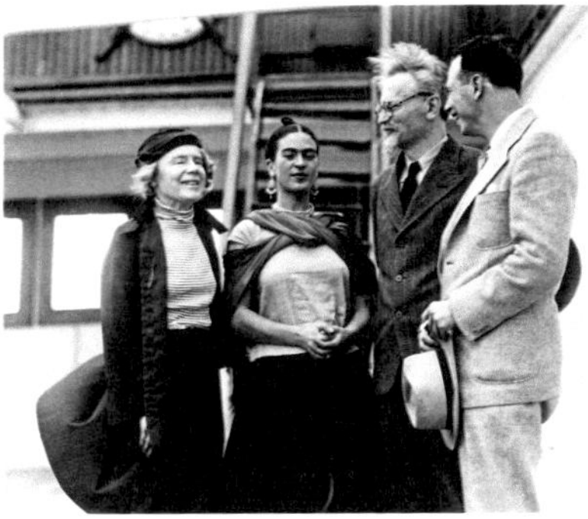

**36** Frida Kahlo and Max Shachtman (right) greet Leon Trotsky (second from right) and his wife (left) at their arrival in Mexico on January 9, 1937

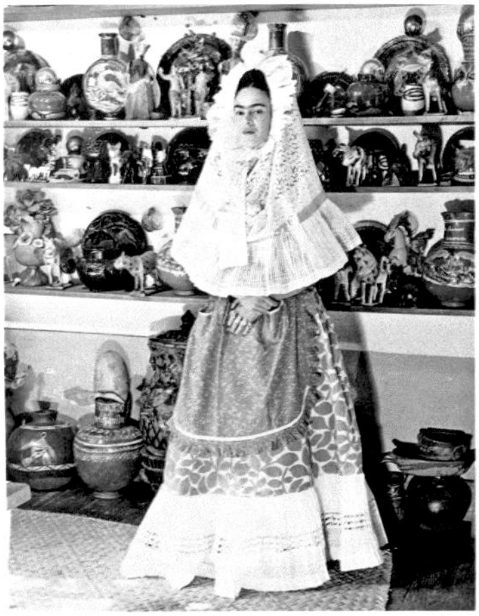

**37** Kahlo, dressed in Tehuana costume, 1940

**1938** Sent by the French Foreign Ministry, André Breton travels to Mexico with his wife Jacqueline. He is enthusiastic about Kahlo's works and praises her as a Surrealist. The gallery owner Julien Levy discovers Kahlo's work in a small group exhibition at the University Gallery in Mexico City. Kahlo's first solo show takes place with twenty-five works in his New York gallery from November 1 to 5. The exhibition is very successful and she sells her first paintings. Kahlo's relationship with the photographer Nickolas Muray begins in New York. She paints the works *Remembrance of the Open Wound*, *What the Water Gave Me* (18), and *Four Inhabitants of Mexico*.

**1939** In Paris, André Breton and Marcel Duchamp pave the way for Frida Kahlo to exhibit at the Renou & Colle Gallery. Among her many admirers are Joan Miró, Wassily Kandinsky, Yves Tanguy, Wolfgang Paalen, and Pablo Picasso. Kahlo leaves San Angel and moves back to the Blue House; she divorces Diego. She paints *The Two Fridas* (3) and the commissioned work *The Suicide of Dorothy Hale*.



**1940** Kahlo participates in the "International Surrealist Exhibition" at the Galería de Arte Mexicano in Mexico City with her only two large-format canvases, *The Two Fridas* (3) and—just completed—*The Wounded Table* (38); the show travels to New York. Further exhibitions follow and Kahlo makes her artistic breakthrough. After an assassination attempt on Leon Trotsky and his later murder, Rivera and Kahlo are suspected of collaboration. The two marry for a second time on Rivera's birthday, December 8, but agree to mutual independence. She paints the works *Self-Portrait with Cropped Hair* (14), *Self-Portrait with Thorn Necklace* (27), and *The Dream* (26).

**1941** Guillermo Kahlo dies on April 14, after which Frida falls into a depression. Rivera moves back to the Blue House. Kahlo becomes a founding member of the Seminario de Cultura Mexicana and participates in the "Modern Mexican Painters" exhibition at the Institute of Modern Art in Boston. She paints her *Self-Portrait with Braid* (23).

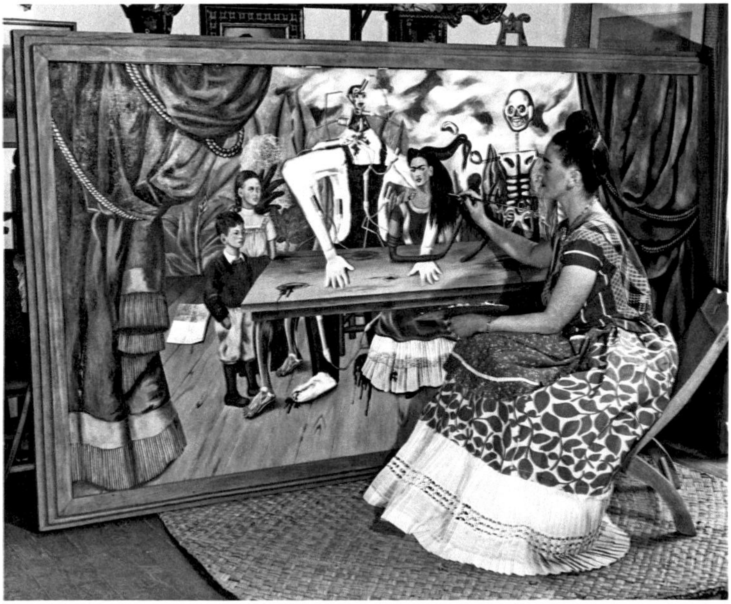

**38** Working on the lost painting *The Wounded Table*, c. 1940

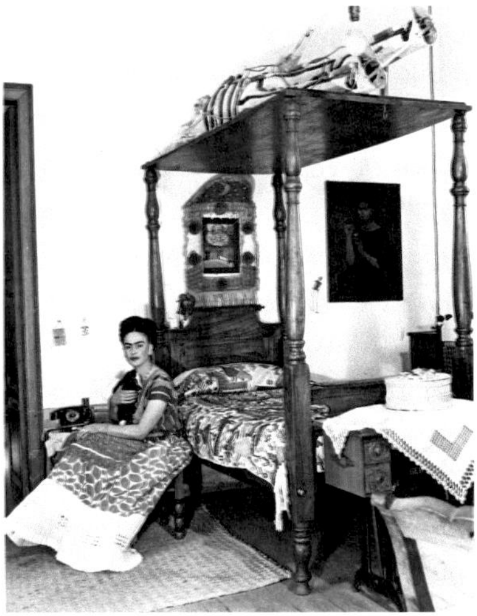

**39** Kahlo in her bedroom, c. 1940

**1942** Construction on the Anahuacalli museum for Rivera's collection of approximately 10,000 pre-Columbian objects begins. Kahlo's works are included among the "20th-Century Portraits" and the "First Papers of Surrealism" shows in New York. In the period between 1942 and 1944 she begins to keep a diary.

**1943** Kahlo participates in the "Exhibition by 31 Women" at Peggy Guggenheim's New York gallery. She begins teaching at La Esmeralda School of painting and sculpture, which opened in 1942; she moves the classes to the Blue House in Coyoacán. Her seven students call themselves "Los Fridos." Kahlo paints *Roots* (30), *Self-Portrait as Tehuana* (15), and *Self-Portrait with Monkeys* (9).

**1944** Kahlo begins the portrait *The Broken Column* and the double portrait *Diego and Frida, 1929–1944* (16). In 1945 she paints *Moses* and *Without Hope*.



**1946** After a bone graft on her spine in New York, Kahlo has to wear a steel corset. She receives a national prize from the Ministry of Education for the painting *Moses*. She creates the works *Tree of Hope* (4) and *The Wounded Deer* (19), as well as a pencil drawing dedicated to Marte R. Gómez with a self-portrait (6).

**1947** Frida, with her *Self-Portrait as Tehuana* (15), is one of four female artists showing works in the exhibition "Forty-Five Self-Portraits by Mexican Painters from the Eighteenth to the Twentieth Century," staged by the National Institute of Fine Arts at the Palacio de Bellas Artes. She paints *Sun and Life* (20) and, the following year, *Self-Portrait (for Samuel Fastlicht)*.

**1949** She participates in the opening of the Mexican Salon of Fine Arts with her just-completed painting *The Love Embrace of the Universe, the Earth (Mexico), Myself, Diego, and Señor Xólotl* (p. 8). For the Rivera retrospective at the Palacio de Bellas Artes in Mexico City, Frida writes the catalogue essay "Portrait of Diego" and creates the double portrait *Diego and I*.

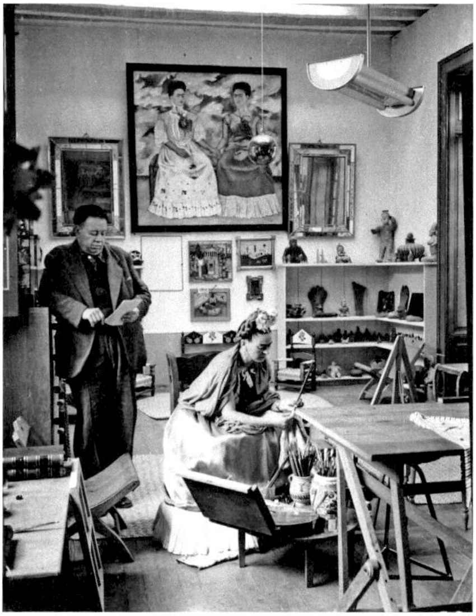

**40** Frida Kahlo and Diego Rivera in their studio, 1948

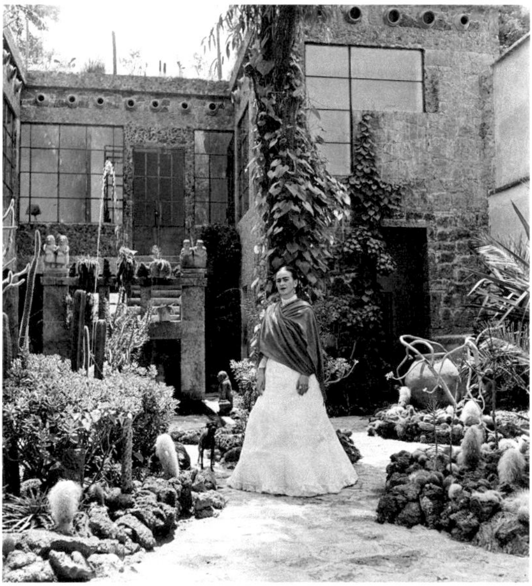

**41** In the garden in Coyoacán, 1951

**1950** After complicated back surgery, Kahlo stays in Mexico City's American Hospital for a full year for six more interventions. She paints *My Family* (29); in 1951 she completes her *Self-Portrait with Portrait of Dr. Farill* (30) and *Portrait of My Father*. In the following years she creates numerous still lifes. Under the influence of drugs and alcohol, her brush-stroke becomes increasingly rough and erratic.

**1953** The first solo exhibition of Kahlo's works in Mexico is a great success—her four-poster bed stands in the middle of Lola Álvarez Bravo's Galería de Arte Contemporáneo. That year her lower right leg has to be amputated, which triggers a growing death wish in her.

**1954** Kahlo's last painting is entitled *Viva la vida (Long Live Life)* (22). On July 2, she takes part in a demonstration for peace in Guatemala, despite having pneumonia. On July 13, 1954, she dies at the Blue House in Coyoacán at the age of 47. It remains unclear whether she commits suicide; officially she dies of a pulmonary embolism.



**1958** The Frida Kahlo Museum is inaugurated in the Blue House in Coyoacán.

**1977** The Mexican government hosts a major Frida Kahlo retrospective at the Palacio de Bellas Artes in Mexico City.

**1984** Frida Kahlo's work is designated part of Mexico's national heritage.

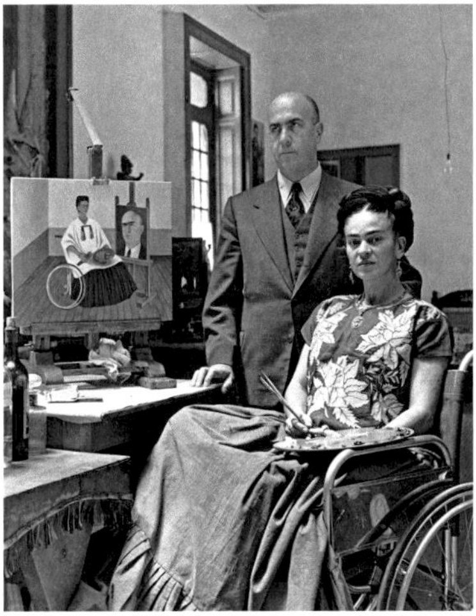

**42** Kahlo with her physician Juan Farill, photographed by Gisèle Freund, Mexico City, 1951

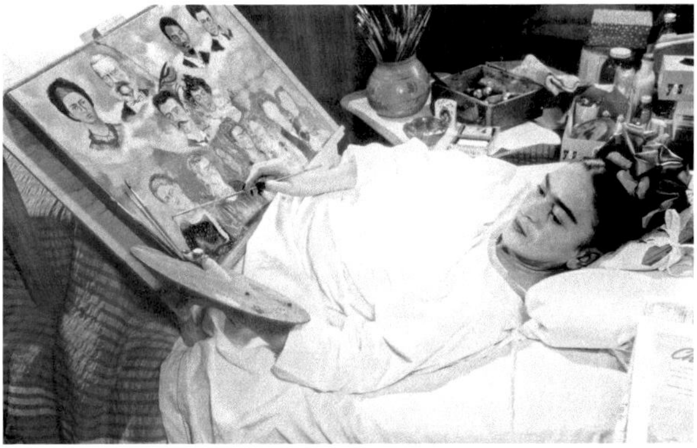

**43** Painting in bed: Kahlo with her work *My Family*, photographed by Juan Guzmán, Mexico City, 1952

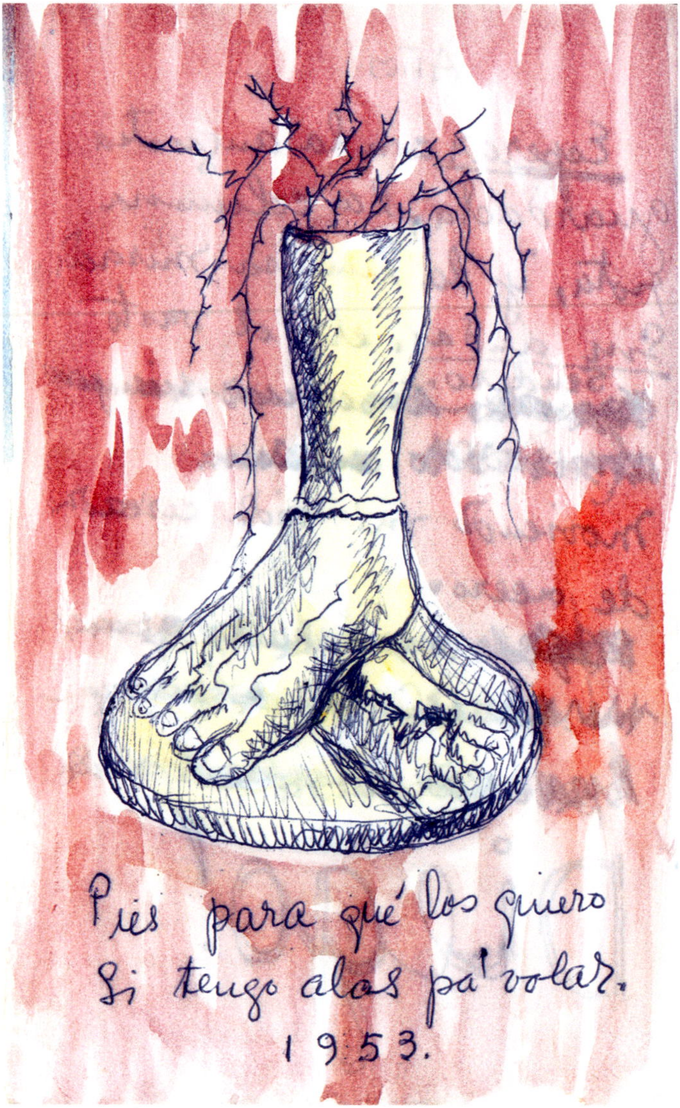


*Pies para qué los quiero. Si tengo alas pa'volar (Feet, what do I need them for when I have wings to fly with)*, 1953, page 134 of Frida Kahlo's diary, 1944–1954, Museo Frida Kahlo, Mexico City

# ARCHIVE

Findings, Documents

1944 – 1954

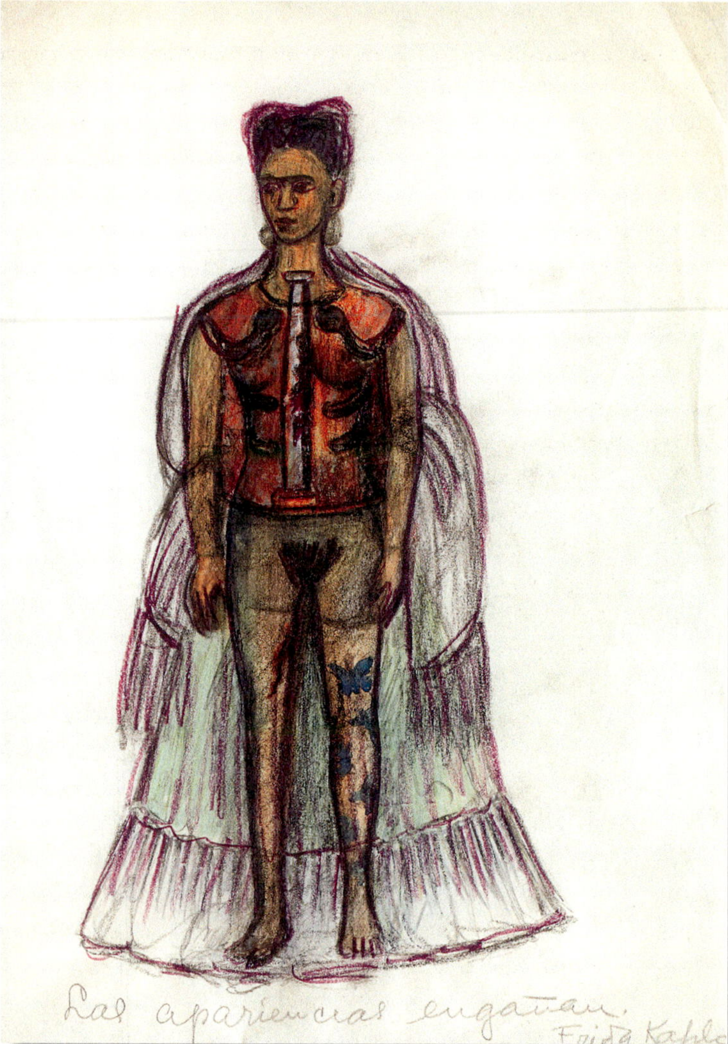


I a

I *Appearances can be Deceiving,* c. 1946, charcoal and colored pencil on paper, 29 × 20.8 cm, Museo Frida Kahlo, Mexico City

I

"I liked to be contradictory." *The answers to the psychological tests that Olga Campos, a friend of the Riveras, conducted from 1949 to 1950 number among the most revealing personal testimonials by Frida Kahlo. Who was this multi-layered person? How did she present herself? What impression did she make on others? Two of her friends remember her:*

*The photographer Gisèle Freund recalls Frida's* "thin, fragile figure" *at their first encounter.* "Dressed in a colorful long silk skirt, she looked like an Aztec princess. [...] Many typical Mexican gold chains were draped around her neck, a 'sarape', a Mexican scarf of red silk, lay over her delicate shoulders. Each finger of her hands was decorated with large, finely engraved rings with precious stones. [...] She smoked, she laughed, she spoke with her warm melodious voice. Her whole personality exuded lively intelligence, a thoroughly humane attitude, and exuberant vitality." *On the back of a photograph, Freund noted that Kahlo was* "a heroic, almost legendary figure of a strange and irresistible beauty."

"She was a high-powered reactor who was constantly discharging," *according to the writer and art critic Raquel Tibol.* "She knew the most profound experience of what we call enthusiasm. She needed the exaltation that is braided into love, joy, and truth. [...] She was suspicious, suspicious of people's passions, hatreds, their peculiarities. She made herself an object of admiration. [...] Frida is a definitive paradox that exemplified the power of rebellion in the face of destiny, [...] of a will shot like an arrow at an adverse destiny."

*It was ultimately Diego Rivera who best summarized the general appreciation for his wife and her work:* "It is the first time in the history of art that a woman has expressed with absolute, stark frankness and, one could say, with tranquil ferocity, the great and small things that exclusively concern women. Her sincerity, which could be described as profoundly tender and cruel at the same time, has led her to bear undeniable, truthful witness to certain things; that is why she has painted her own birth, being breast-fed by her wet nurse, growing up in her family, and her terrible sufferings of all types, without ever exaggerating in the least or deviating from actual events, remaining a realist, profound, as the Mexican people and their art always are, even when she generalizes events and sensations until they achieve a cosmogonic expression. The personal representation of these events and sensations, down to the bare skeleton of

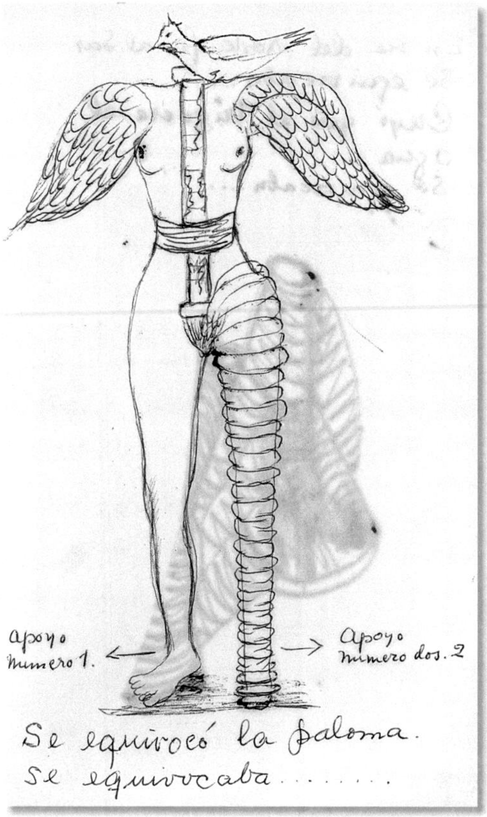


1b

their truth, ensures that the reference to herself acquires, through its accuracy and intensity, a universal level and meaning and a social scope that we could poetically call didactic and rigorously dialectic."

**1b** *Se equivocó la paloma (The Dove was Mistaken),* page 141 of Frida Kahlo's diary, 1944–1954, Museo Frida Kahlo, Mexico City

2

*In 1938 André Breton and his wife, the painter Jacqueline Lamba, made a trip to Mexico. At Lamba's departure Frida Kahlo gave her a present of an oval self-portrait, framed in the form of a butterfly, and below it a small mirror. The picture depicts Kahlo with a corolla and a red ribbon around her throat. Perhaps this gift inspired Breton to his often-quoted comparison, that Frida Kahlo's painting was* "like a ribbon around a bomb."

2

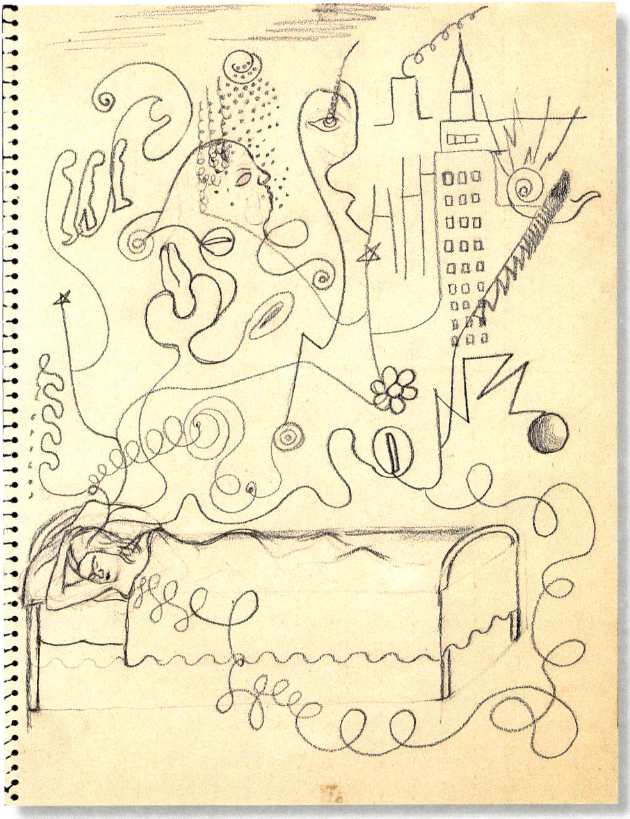

2 *El Loco,* no date, pencil on paper, 25.5 × 18.5 cm, Museo Frida Kahlo, Mexico City

*Surrealism, which arose as a new artistic movement in 1920s Paris, drew on Sigmund Freud's theory of the unconscious and of the dream, standing for the liberation of literature and art from rigid structures. One of its favorite practices was the "écriture automatique," that is, automatic writing. The Surrealists discovered in the traditions, myths, and nature of Mexico fertile ground for their creativity. The oneiric and symbolic power in Kahlo's paintings as well as her intriguing, open, and yet mysterious personality have led to her being grouped together with the Surrealists—a classification which she denied. She did take part, however, in the "Exposición Internacional de Surrealismo" in Inés Amor's Galería de Arte Mexicano in 1940.*

*In his foreword to the catalogue for Frida Kahlo's exhibition at the Julien Levy Gallery 1938, André Breton wrote:* "My surprise and joy was unbounded when I discovered, on my arrival in Mexico, that her work has blossomed forth, in her latest paintings, into pure surreality, despite the fact that it had been conceived without any prior knowledge whatsoever of the ideas motivating the activities of my friends and myself. [...] This art even contains that drop of cruelty and humor uniquely capable of blending the rare affective powers that compound together to form the philtre which is Mexico's secret. The power of inspiration here is nourished by the strange ecstasies of puberty and the mysteries of generation, and, far from considering these to be the mind's private reserves, as in some colder climates, she displays them proudly with a mixture of candour and insolence."

*Kahlo herself commented on her attitude to Surrealism in 1947, in an exhibition catalogue for the Palacio de Bellas Artes:* "I really do not know if my paintings are Surrealist or not, but I do know they are the most frank expression of myself, without ever taking into consideration the judgements nor the prejudices of anyone else. I have painted little, without the least desire of fame or ambition, with the conviction of, above all, pleasing myself, and later being able to earn my living with my work. My travels, during which I saw as much as was possible, wonderful paintings but also very bad ones, have taught me two key things: to try as best as possible to remain true to myself, and the bitter realization that even many lives would never be enough to paint as I wanted to and to paint everything that I wanted."

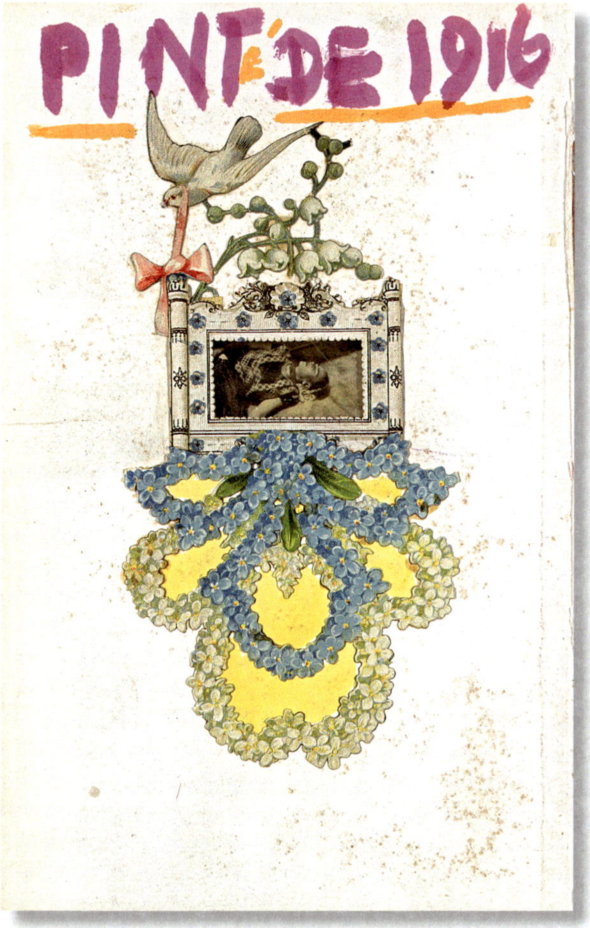


3a

3

*Probably motivated by the death of her father, sometime between 1940 and 1942 Frida Kahlo began to write a diary of associative sketches and texts. It juxtaposed loose groupings of words and letters to others, autobiographical notes, playful ink blots, political as well as artistic commentaries, and long*

---

**3a** *Pinté de 1916 (I painted from 1916 onward)*, page 4 of Frida Kahlo's diary, 1944–54, Museo Frida Kahlo, Mexico City

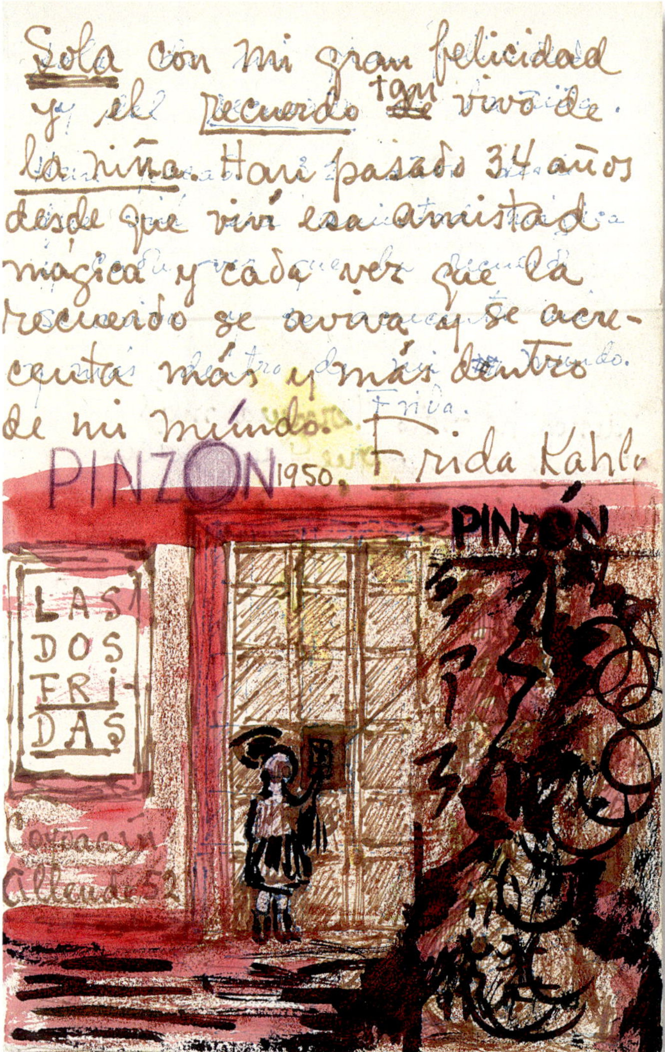


3b

**3b** *Pinzon 1950. Las dos Fridas (The Two Fridas)*, page 85 of Frida Kahlo's diary, 1944–1954, Museo Frida Kahlo, Mexico City

*lists of thank yous, but also numerous painted entries that referred to her physical injuries and despair. The diary ended in 1954, shortly before her death.*

*The title* Pinté de 1916 (I have painted since 1916) *on the diary's first page is surprising, since Frida Kahlo began the diary in the early 1940s. Since she had declared her birth to be in 1910, the year of the Mexican revolution, the entry thus refers to the six-year-old girl Frida, who is portrayed in the diary.*

*In the photograph at the center of the collage Kahlo re-stages herself as a fallen woman. Perhaps it reflects the serious traffic accident that she suffered when she was eighteen; perhaps it prefigures her many, arduous hospital stays, or her death. The original image that served Kahlo as a model belonged to her extensive collection of photographs.*

*On a later diary page, which Kahlo titled* Las Dos Fridas (The Two Fridas), *she describes her imaginary female friend and paints her before the door of the Blue House in Coyoacán.*

# SOURCES



## PICTURE CREDITS

The originals were graciously provided by the museums and collections named in the captions or by the following archives:

akg-images: pp. 17, 19, 38, 39, 42, 53
akg-images / sciencesource / Gisèle Freund: p. 66 top
Alamy: pp. 15, 56
Christie's Images Ltd – ARTOTHEK: pp. 18, 24/25, 26/27
Fine Art Images – ARTOTHEK: pp. 16, 29, 36/37
bpk / IMEC, Fonds MCC / Gisèle Freund: p. 65 bottom
bpk / Schalkwijk/Art Resource, NY: pp. 68, 72, 75, 76
Bridgeman Images: pp. 28, 49, 65 top
Christie's Images / Bridgeman Images: p. 23
Cincinnati Art Museum / Gift of the Artist / Bridgeman Images: pp. 61 bottom, 63 bottom
Detroit Institute of Arts / Founders Society Purchase, Diego Rivera Exhibition Fund / Bridgeman Images: p. 61 top
Detroit Institute of Arts / Gift of the Artist / Bridgeman Images: p. 63 top
Fine Art Images / Bridgeman Images: pp. 8, 10, 20, 30, 33, 35, 44, 61 center
Galerie Bilderwelt / Bridgeman Images: p. 59 bottom
Granger / Bridgeman Images: pp. 59 top, 59 center, 67 bottom
Jorge Contreras Chacel / Bridgeman Images: pp. 46/47
Luisa Ricciarini / Bridgeman Images: p. 14
Sotheby's / Bridgeman Images: pp. 50/51
Galería Arvil: p. 31
Digital image, The Museum of Modern Art, New York / Scala, Florence: p. 12
Photo Schalkwijk /Art Resource/Scala, Florence: pp. 40/41, 52, 73

## LITERATURE USED

Excerpts have been drawn from the following literary sources (identified by page numbers):

p. 72: Salomon Grimberg, *Frida Kahlo. Bekenntnisse* (Munich et al.: 2008), p. 91
pp. 72/73: Gérard de Cortanze (ed.), *Frida Kahlo und Diego Rivera. Gesehen von Gisèle Freund* (Berlin: 2014), pp. 26, 97.
p. 73: Raquel Tibol, *Frida Kahlo – Ein offenes Leben* (Munich: 2005), p. 15.
p. 73: Diego Rivera in an interview with Raquel Tibol, 1953, quoted in: Tibol 2005, p. 145.
p. 74: André Breton, in: exh. cat. Julien Levy Gallery 1938, quoted in: Hayden Herrera, *Frida Kahlo. Ein leidenschaftliches Leben* (Frankfurt am Main: 2008), p. 195.
pp. 74/75: Frida Kahlo, in: *Fünfundvierzig Selbstbildnisse mexikanischer Maler aus dem 18. bis 20. Jahrhundert*, exh. cat. Palacio de Bellas Artes 1947, quoted in: Tibol 2005, p. 148.

Published by
Hirmer Verlag GmbH
Bayerstraße 57–59
80335 Munich
Germany

Cover: *Self-Portrait with Monkeys,* 1943, detail, see p. 43
Double page 2/3: *Still Life (Dedicated to Samuel Fastlicht),* 1951, detail, see p. 39
Double page 4/5: *The Two Fridas,* 1939, detail, see p. 14



www.hirmerpublishers.com

—
**TRANSLATION**
David Sánchez Cano, Madrid

—
**COPY-EDITING**
Jane Michael, Munich

—
**PROJECT MANAGEMENT**
Karen Angne, Rainer Arnold

—
**GRAPHIC DESIGN**
Marion Blomeyer, Rainald Schwarz, Munich

—
**LAYOUT AND PRODUCTION**
Tanja Bokelmann, Munich

—
**PRE-PRESS AND REPRO**
Reproline mediateam GmbH, Munich

—
**PRINTING AND BINDING**
Grafisches Centrum Cuno GmbH & Co. KG, Calbe

Bibliographic information published by the Deutsche Nationalbiliothek. The Deutsche Nationalbibliothek lists this publication in the Deutsche Nationalbibliografie; detailed bibliographic data is available on the Internet at http://dnb.de.

ISBN 978-3-7774-4138-2

Printed in Germany

# ALREADY PUBLISHED

HEINRICH CAMPENDONK
978-3-7774-4084-2

PAUL CÉZANNE
978-3-7774-3813-9

WILLEM DE KOONING
978-3-7774-3073-7

LYONEL FEININGER
978-3-7774-2974-8

CONRAD FELIXMÜLLER
978-3-7774-3824-5

PAUL GAUGUIN
978-3-7774-2854-3

RICHARD GERSTL
978-3-7774-2622-8

JOHANNES ITTEN
978-3-7774-3172-7

VASILY KANDINSKY
978-3-7774-2759-1

FRIDA KAHLO
978-3-7774-4138-2

ERNST LUDWIG KIRCHNER
978-3-7774-2958-8

GUSTAV KLIMT
978-3-7774-3979-2

HENRI MATISSE
978-3-7774-2848-2

PAULA MODERSOHN-BECKER
978-3-7774-3489-6

LÁSZLÓ MOHOLY-NAGY
978-3-7774-3403-2

KOLOMAN MOSER
978-3-7774-3072-0

ALFONS MUCHA
978-3-7774-3488-9

EMIL NOLDE
978-3-7774-2774-4

AGNES PELTON
978-3-7774-3929-7

PABLO PICASSO
978-3-7774-2757-7

HANS PURRMANN
978-3-7774-3679-1

EGON SCHIELE
978-3-7774-2852-9

FLORINE STETTHEIMER
978-3-7774-3632-6

VINCENT VAN GOGH
978-3-7774-2758-4

MARIANNE VON WEREFKIN
978-3-7774-3306-6